Rebecca Morris

Southafternoon

Kunsthalle Lingen

Bonnefantenmuseum Maastricht

Koenig Books, London

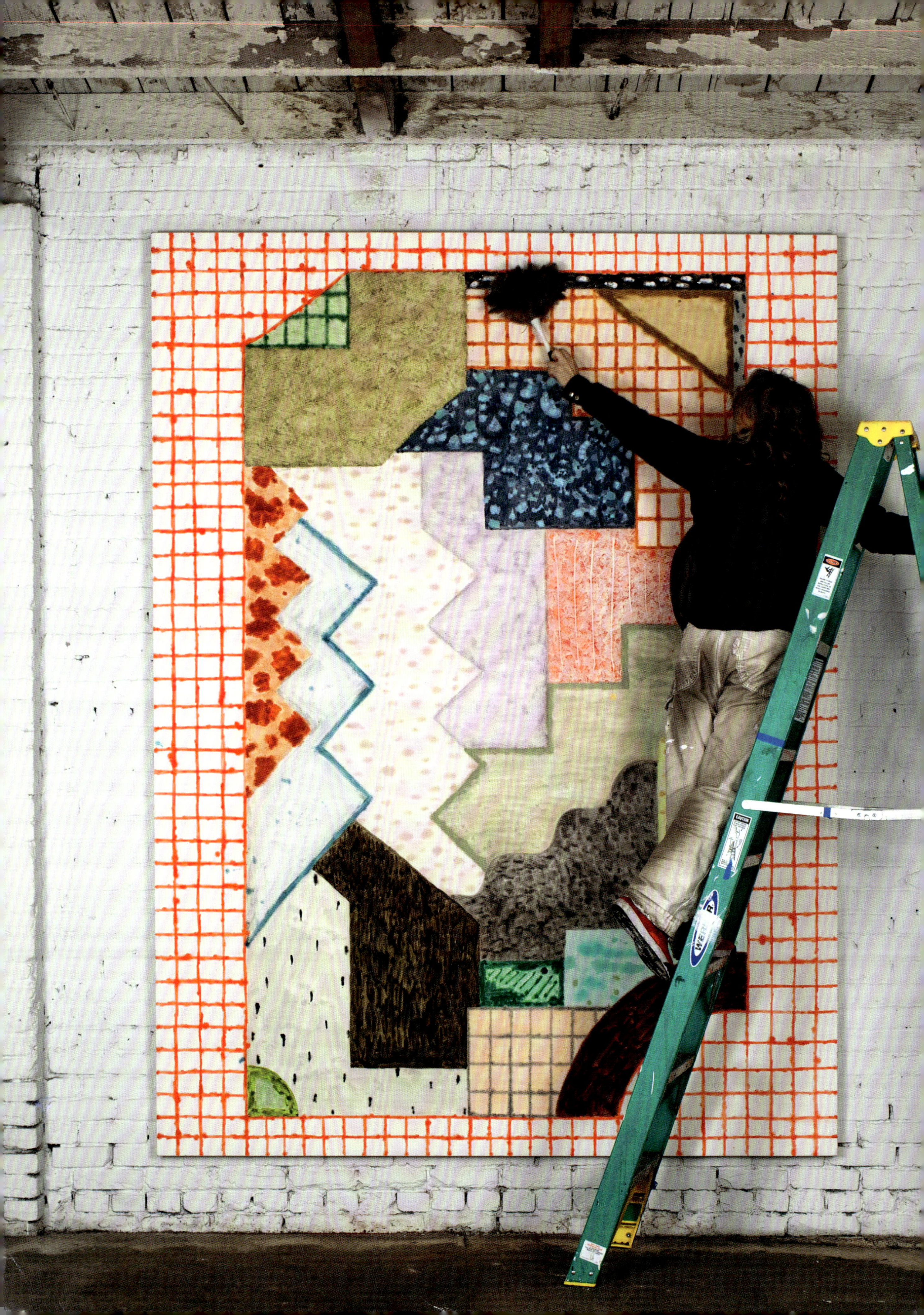

Vorwort

Die Kunsthalle Lingen und das Bonnefantenmuseum Maastricht freuen sich sehr, den vorliegenden Katalog zur Ausstellung *Southafternoon* von Rebecca Morris präsentieren zu können. Ihre ersten institutionellen Einzelausstellungen in Deutschland und den Niederlanden begleitend, hoffen wir mit dieser Veröffentlichung dazu beitragen zu können, ein neues Publikum an das außergewöhnliche Werk der Künstlerin heranzuführen. Es soll an dieser Stelle die Möglichkeit der vertieften Auseinandersetzung mit einer malerischen Praxis geschaffen werden, die sich durch eine gänzlich eigene Auffassung von Abstraktion charakterisiert.

In seiner formalen und inhaltlichen Offenheit und Vielschichtigkeit belebt die Malerei von Rebecca Morris die Institutionen auf besondere Art und Weise und erscheint in der Architektur des Bonnefantenmuseums Maastricht und der Kunsthalle Lingen in je eigenem Licht und eigener Akzentuierung. Für das Bonnefantenmuseum Maastricht als Institution mit eigener Sammlung ist es von besonderer Bedeutung mit *Southafternoon* eine weitere Ausstellung realisieren zu können, die organisch an die Entwicklung der bisherigen Sammlungsgeschichte anschließt und einen Beitrag zu deren Fortsetzung leistet. So können sich die ausgestellten Malereien und Zeichnungen in Teilen der Bonnefanten-Kollektion spiegeln, zugleich aber auch selbst neue Perspektiven offenbaren. Rebecca Morris' eigenwillige Abstraktionen beziehen in vielfältiger Weise Stellung zu Protagonisten der Sammlung des Museums und finden in den Arbeiten von Mary Heilmann, Monika Baer und Laura Owens – um nur einige Beispiele zu nennen – einen wichtigen Kontext. Eine solche konstruktive Begegnung hoffen das Bonnefantenmuseum Maastricht und die Kunsthalle Lingen ihrerseits mit Blick auf eine jüngere Generation abstrakter Malerinnen und Maler zu ermöglichen. Rebecca Morris abstrahiert in ihren Arbeiten nicht von konkreten Gegenständen oder anderen Referenzen; vielmehr wird durch selbstreflexive Gesten und den Verzicht auf konkrete Titel eine Offenheit gegenüber Interpretationsansätzen erreicht. Gerade in dieser Zugänglichkeit der Werke von Rebecca Morris liegt eine ihrer Qualitäten, sie fordern zu einem Dialog zwischen Werk und Betrachter heraus, der niemals zu enden scheint, gibt es doch in den Arbeiten immer wieder Unergründliches zu entdecken.

Für die erfolgreiche Zusammenarbeit zwischen den beiden Häusern im Vorfeld der Ausstellungen und bei der Realisierung des Katalogs wollen wir uns bei allen Beteiligten ganz herzlich bedanken, insbesondere natürlich bei Rebecca Morris, die *Southafternoon* mit großem Engagement in allen Phasen begleitete. Die Ausstellung und die Publikation hätten ebenfalls nicht realisiert werden können ohne die Hilfe und Unterstützung zahlreicher weiterer Personen. Wir danken vor allem der Galerie Barbara Weiss und hier insbesondere Barbara Weiss, Kirsten Wandschneider, Christina Green und Daniel Herleth. Weiterhin gilt unser herzlicher Dank den Autorinnen Corrina Peipon, Kuratorin am Hammer Museum in Los Angeles, und Paula van den Bosch, Kuratorin des Bonnefantenmuseums Maastricht, für ihre erhellenden und bezugsreichen Texte. Ein ganz besonderer Dank gilt auch Knut Wiese für die Gestaltung dieses Katalogs.

Stijn Huijts
Direktor Bonnefantenmuseum Maastricht

Meike Behm
Direktorin Kunsthalle Lingen

Preface

The Kunsthalle Lingen and the Bonnefantenmuseum Maastricht are delighted to be able to present this catalogue for the *Southafternoon* exhibition of works by Rebecca Morris. We hope that this publication, as an accompaniment to her first institutional solo exhibitions in Germany and the Netherlands, will help bring Morris's exceptional work to a new audience. This catalogue is intended to create an opportunity for deeper engagement with a painterly practice that is distinguished by an utterly unique approach to abstraction.

The openness and complexity of the form and content of Rebecca Morris's paintings invigorates the exhibition spaces in a special way, appearing in a different light and differently accentuated in interplay with the respective architecture of the Bonnefantenmuseum Maastricht and the Kunsthalle Lingen. For the Bonnefantenmuseum Maastricht as an institution with its own collection, *Southafternoon* is especially significant as a chance to organically continue with the history of the collection and to help further its development. The exhibited paintings and drawings can reflect parts of the Bonnefanten collection, also open up new perspectives. Rebecca Morris's idiosyncratic abstractions resonate with the museum collection's protagonists in many different ways, and in particular context can be found in works by Mary Heilmann, Monika Baer and Laura Owens, to name just a few examples. The Bonnefantenmuseum Maastricht and the Kunsthalle Lingen also hope to foster such a constructive encounter between Morris's oeuvre and a younger generation of abstract painters. Rebecca Morris does not abstract from concrete objects or other reference points in her works. Rather, her self-reflexive gestures and eschewing of concrete titles achieve a certain openness of interpretive approach. The approachability of Morris's works is one of their virtues, provoking a dialogue between the work and the observer that seems never to end, as there are always further depths to be plumbed.

We would like to extend our most heartfelt thanks to all those involved for the excellent collaboration between the two institutions in the run-up to the exhibition and in the creation of the catalogue. Of course, we especially thank Rebecca Morris, who has shown great dedication at every phase of *Southafternoon*. The exhibition and this publication also would not have been possible without the help and support of many other people. Special thanks to the Barbara Weiss Gallery, especially to Barbara Weiss, Kirsten Wandschneider, Christina Green and Daniel Herleth. And thank you very much to contributing authors Corrina Peipon, curator at the Hammer Museum in Los Angeles, and Paula van den Bosch, curator at the Bonnefantenmuseum Maastricht, for their illuminating and evocative texts. We are also particularly grateful to Knut Wiese for designing this catalogue.

Stijn Huijts
Director Bonnefantenmuseum Maastricht

Meike Behm
Director Kunsthalle Lingen

Meike Behm

Der Fluss der Dinge

Zum ersten Mal begegnete ich den Werken von Rebecca Morris im Rahmen einer Einzelausstellung, *Shards and Skywindows,* in der Galerie von Barbara Weiss in Berlin im Jahr 2009. Dort präsentierte sie großformatige Abstraktionen neben einer Serie aus kleineren, dreieckigen Gemälden, jeweils ohne Titel. Schon damals beeindruckten die Bilder von Rebecca Morris durch ihren malerisch explizit formulierten Anspruch auf Eigenständigkeit, einhergehend mit einem bewussten Einbezug ihrer historischen Verankerung. Gestische Elemente, wie sie aus dem Abstrakten Expressionismus oder dem Informel bekannt sind, aber auch eher konzeptuelle Momente, wie sie für die Abstraktion der 1960er und 1970er Jahre kennzeichnend sind, traten Seite an Seite auf und wurden von Morris in einer Malerei verbunden, die sich als lebendiges, dynamisches System zeigte. Es war vor allem diese Offenheit innerhalb der Abstraktion, die Verbindung von kunstimmanenten Bezugssystemen mit einem großen Repertoire an malerischen Mitteln, die mich seit damals am Werk von Rebecca Morris faszinierten.

Dicht gesetzte Farbformen auf dunklem Grund wechselten sich ab mit großzügiger auf hellem Grund angeordneten, einige Bereiche ließen figurative Assoziationen zu, aber kaum war es gelungen, eine scheinbare Eindeutigkeit abzulesen, löste sich diese beim Anblick einer weiteren Form zugunsten einer Vieldeutigkeit auf. Der Verzicht auf konkrete Titel trug zu einer spannungsvollen Ambivalenz der Bilder bei, Interpretationen konnten sich sowohl in gegenständlichen als auch in abstrakten Bereichen bewegen. Selbst bei intensiver Betrachtung schien es unmöglich, eine in sich stimmige Deutung abzulesen, die nicht sofort wieder von einer alternativen Lesart in Frage gestellt worden wäre. Für ihre Einzelausstellung in der Kunsthalle Lingen entschieden wir, uns auf jüngere Malereien zu konzentrieren, gemeinsam mit einer Auswahl an Arbeiten, die vor 2012 entstanden waren, und von einer Serie von Arbeiten auf Papier. Auf die offene Struktur der Architektur der Kunsthalle bezugnehmend, schien es nur natürlich, die Bilder nicht chronologisch zu hängen, sondern sie in assoziative Nachbarschaften zu gruppieren, die auf verschiedenen Ebenen Beziehungen zwischen den einzelnen Arbeiten herzustellen erlaubten. Auf Stellwänden arrangiert, die den Raum in verschiedene Bereiche gliederten, griffen diese ein vertrautes Motiv aus Morris' Malerei auf: Zick-Zack-förmige Linien finden sich wiederholt in ihren Kompositionen, sie vermitteln einen Eindruck von einer Praxis, die sich einfachen Zuschreibungen verweigert, und bilden eine räumliche Chiffre für ihre Malerei. Die neueren Werke von Rebecca Morris bestehen aus einer Serie von eher kargen und formreduzierten Formen auf weißem Grund, die allerdings komplexe Binnenstrukturen aufweisen. Bezogen auf diese Arbeiten, spricht Rebecca Morris selbst von Mini-Gemälden unterschiedlicher Stilrichtungen, die auf einer einzigen Leinwand miteinander vereint werden. In gewisser Weise, so Morris, bilden diese Arbeiten in ihrer Gegenüberstellung von kleineren und kontrastierenden internen Elementen innerhalb eines Gesamtbildes einen formalen Geschmacks- und Gleichgewichtstest, der herausfordert und animiert.

Rebecca Morris arbeitet meist gleichzeitig an mehreren Bildern. Dabei löst sie teilweise Elemente aus ihren Bildern heraus, entwickelt sie individuell weiter und setzt diese dann neu zusammen. Dieser Entstehungsprozess könnte mit dem Begriff des Zitierens, des Selbstzitats, beschrieben werden – oder besser mit demjenigen des Abstrahierens?

Bei Morris bewegt sich das Phänomen der Abstraktion immer im Bereich der Selbstreflektion und des Feldes der Malerei selbst. Diese wird nicht eingesetzt, um fertige Zustände zu schildern; eher lässt sie eine wohlbedachte Mischung aus Intuition, Rationalität und subjektivem Ausdruck erkennen. Zwischen den Bildelementen, den Werken und ihren Betrachterinnen und Betrachtern entsteht ein kommunikativer Diskurs, der sich nie zugunsten einer finalen Entscheidung auflöst.

Meike Behm

The Flow of Things

I first encountered Rebecca Morris's work at her solo exhibition, *Shards and Skywindows*, at Barbara Weiss's gallery in Berlin in 2009. In this exhibition, she presented large-scale abstract works alongside a series of smaller triangular paintings, all untitled. Even then, in these pictures, Morris's way of painting already impressively formulated an explicit claim to independence that went hand in hand with a deliberate inclusion of the historical moorings of her work. Gestural elements familiar from Abstract Expressionism or Informalism appeared side-by-side with conceptual touches evocative of 1960s and 70s abstraction; Morris fused these elements into paintings that appeared as a dynamic living system. This openness within abstraction, this connection of artistic frames of reference with a broad repertoire of painting techniques, is what has fascinated me about Rebecca Morris's work ever since.

Colored shapes arranged densely against a dark background alternated with others placed more spaciously against a light background: in some places figurative associations were possible, but just as soon as a seemingly legible form took clear shape, another glimpse revealed a different shape, dissolving it into ambiguity. The paintings' lack of specific titles added to the tension of their ambivalence; interpretative possibilities opened up in both representational and abstract areas. Even after intense observation, it felt impossible to reach any internally cohesive interpretation that was not immediately called into question by an alternative reading. For Morris's solo exhibition at the Kunsthalle Lingen we decided to focus on her more recent paintings, with a selection of some works from before 2012, as well as a series of works on paper. Given the Kunsthalle's open architectural structure, it seemed only natural to group the works into associative neighborhoods, which allowed for relationships to form among them at multiple levels, rather than hanging them chronologically. The pictures were arranged on movable walls that divided the space into different areas, and echoed a familiar motif of Morris's work: zigzag lines. These appear recurrently in her compositions, conveying the impression of a practice that denies itself any simple attributions and forming a spatial cypher for her paintings. Rebecca Morris's newer works comprise a series of shapes against a white background; these are rather austere and minimal in form but nonetheless display complex internal structures. Morris herself speaks of these works as mini-paintings in different styles that are brought together on a single canvas. In a certain sense, according to Morris, these works' juxtaposition of smaller and contrasting internal elements within a total image creates a formal test of taste and balance, which is both challenging and stimulating.

Rebecca Morris generally works on multiple paintings at the same time. In doing so she separates out certain elements from her pictures, develops them further individually, and combines them anew. This creative process could be described as one of citation, self-citation or, perhaps better yet, abstraction. With Morris, the phenomenon of abstraction always operates within the realm of self-reflection and the field of painting itself. It is not deployed to depict finished conditions, but rather evokes a well-considered mixture of intuition, rationality and subjective expression. What emerges in-between the figurative elements, the works and their observers is a communicative discourse that never resolves itself into a final decision.

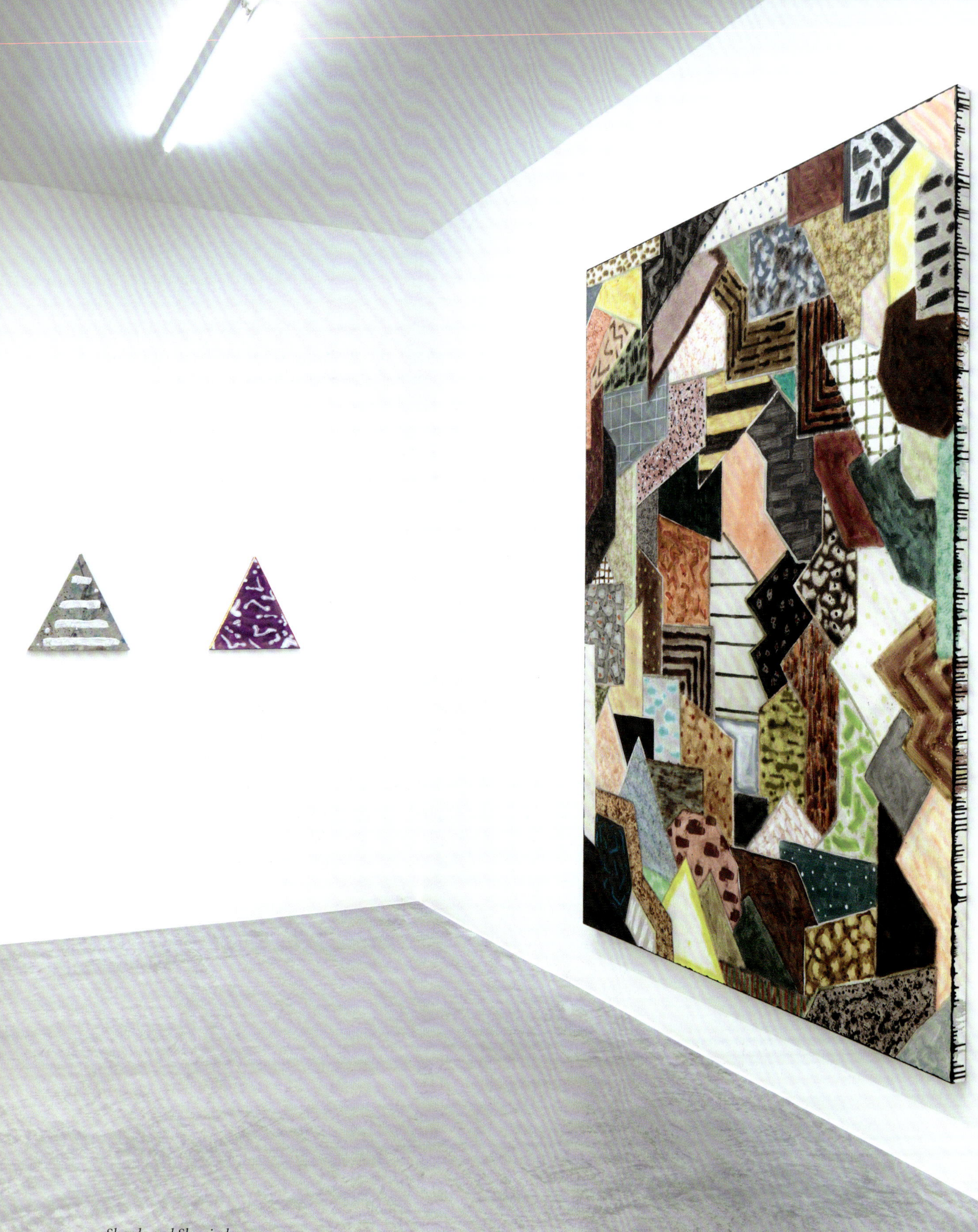

Shards and Skywindows
Ausstellungsansicht / Installation view
Galerie Barbara Weiss, Berlin, 2009

Paula van den Bosch

Old School / New School

Unlängst wurde ich in einem Berliner Museum geradezu überwältigt von dem großartigen Werk der Schwedin Hilma af Klint (1862–1944), vermutlich die erste Pionierin der abstrakten Kunst. In ihrem Testament, so las ich, hatte Klint verfügt, dass ihr Œuvre erst zwanzig Jahre nach ihrem Tod ausgestellt werden dürfe. Sie nahm wohl an, dass die tatsächliche Bedeutung ihrer spirituellen Abstraktion ihren Zeitgenossen verborgen geblieben wäre: Klint malte Bilder für die Zukunft. Unwillkürlich musste ich an Rebecca Morris denken, jedenfalls an einen merkwürdigen Passus aus ihrem 1994 verfassten Manifest mit dem Titel *MANIFESTO (For Abstractionists and Friends of the Non-Objective)*, der wie Grundsatzerklärung und Hilfeschrei zusammen klingt: „Make work that is so secret, so fantastic, so dramatically old school / new school that it looks like it was found in a shed, locked up since the 1940's."

Es ist bekannt, dass es seit längerer Zeit eine Skepsis gegenüber der Malerei gibt. Seit den 1980er-Jahren wurde der Diskurs über Postmoderne und theoretische Koordinaten geführt und ein einflussreicher Teil von Kritikern der Kunstwelt hatte das bewährte Medium mit dem Vorwurf ins Abseits gedrängt, dass es als handwerkliches Ausdrucksmittel ein Anachronismus geworden sei. Dieser postmoderne Bildersturm scheint sich inzwischen ausgewütet zu haben. Die technologische Entwicklung führte zu einer nahezu totalen Virtualisierung der realen Welt. Damit wurden die Wiederverwendung von Bildern und Zeichen sowie das Nachdenken über die Art und Weise unseres Umgangs mit diesen Abbildungen zur Konvention. Die jüngste Generation Künstler beschäftigt sich nicht mehr mit dem Verlust der Herkunft und der Erfahrung der realen Welt, sondern sucht – ohne jeden Zynismus – nach Arbeitsweisen, um offen und bedingungslos mit recycelten Bildern als einzigem Horizont unserer Realität fortfahren zu können. Ein wichtiger Bezugspunkt für diese Generation ist, wie könnte es auch anders sein, die *old school / new school* Abstraktion von Rebecca Morris.

Seit zwanzig Jahren hält Morris an ihrem individuellen Kurs fest. Sie entwickelte eine abstrakte Bildsprache, die über die modernen Traditionen, etwa den Modernismus, die Pop Art oder die Urban Culture, hinausgeht und in welcher handwerkliches Können und Materie erneut eine Hauptrolle einfordern. Morris bedient sich in ihren Darstellungen einer Ikonografie fragmentierter und zersplitterter abstrakter Formen, aus denen sie neue Konstellationen bildet. Manchmal ähnelt dies losgeschlagenen Eisschollen, forttreibend in einem monochromen oder pointillistischen Kontinuum, oder aufgequollenen Vermicelli, die in einer Ursuppe versinken. Ein Jahrhundert Abstraktion marschiert an uns vorbei: Russischer Konstruktivismus; Bauhaus; Orphischer Kubismus; ‚Materiemalerei'; Keith Haring und die Subkultur des Graffiti; sogar Po-Mo-Design. Doch diese Aufzählung spielt eigentlich keine Rolle, denn Morris zieht, ihrem Medium vertrauend, eine tiefe Furche in die materiellen und technischen Eigenschaften der Malerei. Sie benutzt jeden technischen Trick und spielt mit Farbe, die sie auf die Leinwand bürstet, gießt, reibt, sprüht oder auftürmt.

Äußerst raffiniert ist auch ihr Umgang mit der Wirkung der Materialien, der Inkonsistenz von Textur, den unterschiedlichen Trocknungszeiten, dem Gegensatz von Transparenz und Mattheit sowie der Farbtonalität in verschiedenen Farbsorten. Dadurch kommt nicht die Ikonografie, sondern die materielle Schichtung der Darstellung zum Ausdruck. Alte Bekannte, vom Spiritismus bis hin zum Untergrund, räsonieren auch weiterhin. Doch weil Morris ihren eigenen Regeln folgt, gelingt es ihr frisch und vital aus dieser ‚Materialschlacht' der Kunstgeschichte hervorzugehen.

Der Herstellungsprozess steht bei Morris im Mittelpunkt; ihr Leitprinzip ist nicht ein Programm oder eine Theorie, sondern Improvisation. Das erfordert sowohl Talent als auch technisches Können und Hingabe. Morris' Arbeiten auf Papier zeugen hiervon. Jeden Tag, Jahr für Jahr, erprobt und verinnerlicht sie, unter anderem mit ihren persönlichen Initialen als Versuchsfeld, ein Repertoire gemalter Gesten, um auf diese Weise ihren abstrakten Darstellungen eine trügerische Nonchalance und entspannte Stimmung zu verleihen. Sie selbst nennt es „hardboiled abstraction". Morris' großes Vorbild ist, in jeder Hinsicht, der belgische abstrakte Maler Raoul De Keyser (1930–2012), in dessen offenem und mäanderndem Formalismus – das Ergebnis der bedingungslosen Hingabe an sein Metier – das Leben selbst mitzuschwingen scheint.

Als nach 1964 das Werk Hilma af Klints öffentlich zugänglich wurde, ließ die Anerkennung ihrer Vorreiterrolle noch Jahrzehnte auf sich warten. Gender spielte hierbei eine Rolle und tut es übrigens noch immer. Obschon Klint eine wichtige Wegbereiterin war, fand Morris' Auseinandersetzung in den letzten zwanzig Jahren auf einer anderen Bühne statt. Als Studentin wurde sie mit postmodernen Kunsttheorien überschwemmt, das Malen fand kaum Beachtung und Wertschätzung. Die Spuren dieser jahrzehntelang auferlegten theoretischen Unterdrückung sind nicht ohne weiteres auszulöschen. Dies illustriert der Schock, den die junge Künstlerin empfand, als sie in Übersichtsausstellungen mit Werken Piet Mondrians und Robert Rymans konfrontiert wurde. Im Jahre 2012 sagt sie hierüber: „Seeing that work opened up to me what abstraction was: it was that simple. I had been overthinking it, making it too hard (…)."

Hilma af Klint glaubte an eine bessere Zukunft. Ihre Selbstverbannung aus dem Diskurs mag heute naiv und zugleich anmaßend wirken. Auch Rebecca Morris scheute sich nicht in einem öffentlichen Manifest über ein „back to the future"-Szenarium für ihr Werk nachzudenken. Es ist einfach, sich darüber abfällig zu äußern, doch genau daraus entsteht Kunst, und das berührt und fasziniert mich und es regt mich immer wieder zum Nachdenken an.

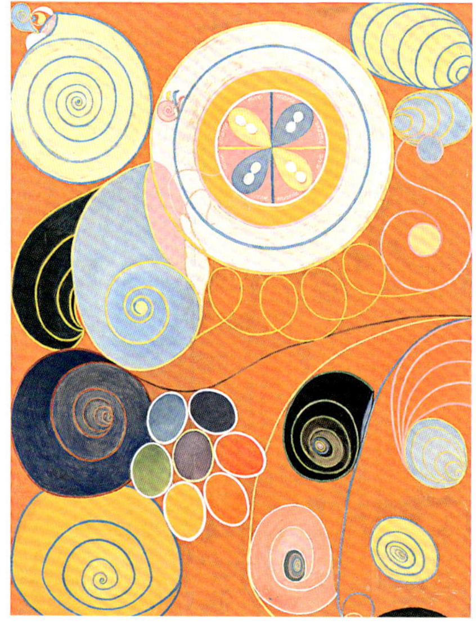

Hilma af Klint, *The Ten Largest, No. 3 Youth, Group IV*, 1907
Tempera auf Papier, aufgezogen auf Leinwand / Tempera on paper mounted on canvas
321 × 240 cm / 126½ × 94½ in

Mit Dank an:
Stephen Westfall und Diedrich Diederichsen, Rebecca Morris: Paintings 1996–2005, Chicago, Renaissance Society at the University of Chicago, 2005.
Gregory Salzman (u. a.), Raoul De Keyser: 1980–1999, Ludion, Ghent (BE), 2000.

Paula van den Bosch

Old School / New School

Recently, at a museum in Berlin, I was blown away by the masterful work of Swedish artist Hilma af Klint (1862–1944), perhaps the first pioneer of abstract art. I read that Klint had stated in her will that her oeuvre should not be made public until at least twenty years after her death. The true significance of her spiritual abstraction would only elude her contemporaries: Klint was painting pictures for the future. I could not help but think of Rebecca Morris, or at least of a curious sentence in her 1994 *MANIFESTO (For Abstractionists and Friends of the Non-Objective)*, which sounds like both a statement of principles and a cry of distress: "Make work that is so secret, so fantastic, so dramatically old school/new school that it looks like it was found in a shed, locked up since the 1940s."

It has often been pointed out that, for a long time, the art world's attitude towards painting was not exactly friendly. From the 1980s, the discourse revolved around postmodern and theoretical issues, and an influential contingent of critics marginalised this time-honoured, traditional medium, accusing it of having become an anachronism. That postmodern iconoclasm appears to have run its course, and in the meantime technological developments have resulted in an almost total virtualisation of reality. Re-use of pictures and signs has become a convention, as has reflection upon our consumption of such images. The youngest generation of artists is no longer concerned with the loss of the source and the experience of the real, but is searching—without a trace of cynicism—for approaches that will allow them openly and unconditionally to continue working with recycled images as the sole horizon of our reality. Rebecca Morris's *old school/new school* abstraction naturally serves as a beacon for this generation.

Over the past twenty years, Morris has resolutely trodden her own path, developing an abstract visual language that transcends modern traditions such as Modernism, Pop Art and urban culture, with craftsmanship and material once again playing a leading role. In her work, Morris employs an iconography of fragmented and splintered abstract shapes that form new constellations. Sometimes they resemble ice floes drifting within a monochromatic or pointillist continuum, or swollen vermicelli sinking in a primordial soup. A century of abstraction files past: Russian Constructivism; Bauhaus; Orphic Cubism; material painting, Keith Haring and the subculture of graffiti; even PoMo design. But this line-up is actually irrelevant; Morris, with complete confidence in her medium, leaves her own deep trace within the material and technical aspects of painting. She employs every technical trick, playing with paint, brushing, pouring, rubbing, spraying, and laying it like bricks onto the canvas. She also makes skilful use of the properties of the materials; the inconsistencies in the texture; the range of drying times; transparency versus opacity; and colour tonality in different types of paint. As a result, it is not the iconography, but the multi-layered material nature of the work that finds expression. Old acquaintances, from Spiritualism to the underground, continue to resonate, but Morris, always working on her own terms, succeeds in emerging from the 'Materialschlacht' of art history with freshness and vitality.

The process of making is central to Morris's work; her guiding principle is not a programme or a theory, but improvisation. This requires not only talent but also technical skill and dedication, as can be seen in Morris's works on paper. Day in, day out, year after year, Morris uses subjects including her own initials as a practice ground, testing and internalising a repertoire of painted gestures, in order to lend a deceptive nonchalance and relaxed atmosphere to her abstract depictions. Morris herself calls it "hardboiled abstraction." Her role model, in every respect, is the Belgian abstract painter Raoul De Keyser (1930–2012), in whose open and meandering formalism—the result of unconditional devotion to his craft—life itself appears to resonate.

Recognition of Hilma af Klint's role as a pioneer, after her work became public in 1964, was decades in coming. Gender played a part in this, and continues to do so. Although Klint is an important predecessor for her, Morris's battle of the past twenty years has taken place within a different arena. As a student, Morris was bombarded with postmodern art theories; painting was rarely taken seriously. The traces left by those decades of immersion in theory cannot simply be erased, as illustrated, for example, by Morris's confrontation with retrospective exhibitions of work by Piet Mondrian and Robert Ryman. As an artist who was just starting out, it came as a shock to her: In 2012, she remarked that, "Seeing that work opened up to me what abstraction was: it was that simple. I had been overthinking it, making it too hard (...)."

Hilma af Klint believed in a better future. Her self-imposed exile from the discourse may now seem somewhat naive and even pretentious. In her public manifesto, too, Rebecca Morris has not shied away from fantasising about a "back to the future" scenario for her own work. It may be easy to scoff, but this is where art comes from, and that is something that touches me, fascinates me and constantly keeps me thinking.

Thanks to:
Stephen Westfall and Diedrich Diederichsen, Rebecca Morris: Paintings 1996–2005, Chicago, Renaissance Society at the University of Chicago, 2005.
Gregory Salzman, (and others), Raoul De Keyser: 1980–1999, Ludion, Ghent (BE), 2000.

Southafternoon
Ausstellungsansicht / Installation view
Kunsthalle Lingen, Lingen, 2013

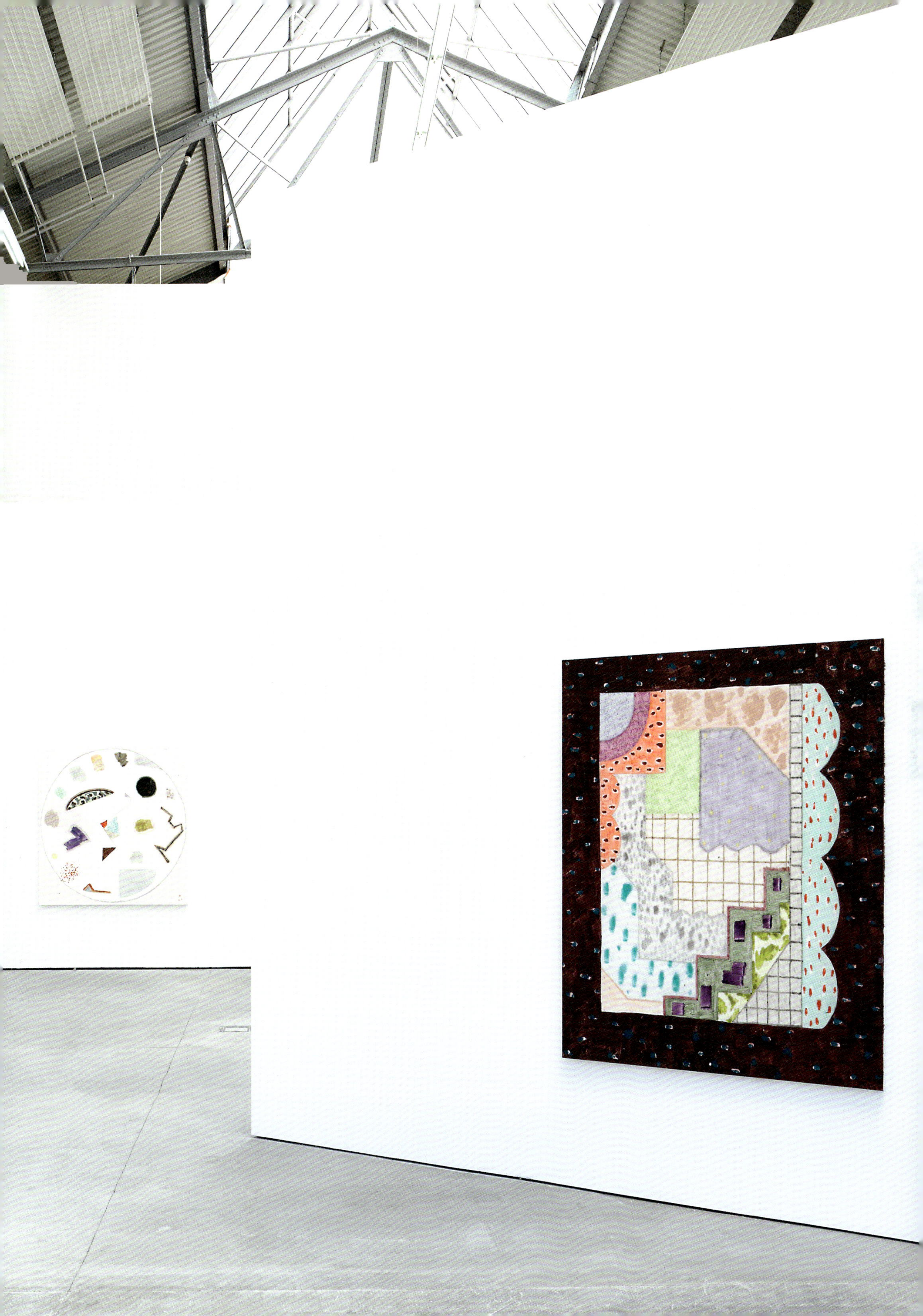

Corrina Peipon

Hi.

Kürzlich besuchte ich Rebecca Morris in ihrem Atelier, weil ich eine bessere Vorstellung davon bekommen wollte, wie das für sie ist, ihre Bilder zu malen. Ich wollte meine eigene Wahrnehmung ihrer Bilder vom Standpunkt des Betrachters aus mit dem in Einklang bringen, was sie sieht, was sie ausdrücken möchte und wie sie ihre Arbeiten entstehen lässt. Bei meiner Ankunft bat mich die Künstlerin, ihr kurz zur Hand zu gehen. Gemeinsam stellten wir eins ihrer am Boden liegenden Gemälde aufrecht hin und traten dann ein paar Schritte zurück, um all ihre neuen Bilder zu betrachten, die an den Wänden lehnten. Auf dem Boden verstreut waren wie immer Schutzhüllen, Klebeband und Pappschalen voll mit verschiedenen Farben und Pinseln. Rebecca Morris sagte, ich müsste nicht darauf achten, wohin ich träte. Ich blickte auf meine Füße und auf die Schälchen mit den Farben überall, und ich sah den leeren Platz, an dem vor meiner Ankunft das Gemälde gelegen hatte, das wir gerade eben aufgestellt hatten. Als ich meinen Blick dann wieder auf die Bilder richtete, wirkten sie plötzlich ganz anders, und mir war, als könnte ich etwas, das ich schon sehr lange Zeit betrachtete, nun endlich richtig *sehen*.

Rebecca Morris arbeitet fast ausschließlich auf dem Boden. Sie legt ihn mit Papier oder Leinwand aus und macht diese Materialien bisweilen auch zur Grundlage neuer Gemälde. Sie legt ihre Keilrahmen einfach darüber und legt los. Da Rebecca Morris bei der Arbeit über ihren Bildern steht, kann sie sich ihnen von allen Seiten nähern und die Leinwand von jeder Seite, aus jedem Winkel, aus jeder Richtung bearbeiten. Es gibt kein Oben und kein Unten, kein Links und kein Rechts, sie muss sich keinem Richtungszwang beugen. Die Gemälde gleichen Luftaufnahmen ihrer eigenen Entstehung, sie sind wie ein Kompass, der sich unablässig neu einnordet. Ich habe dabei den Eindruck, dass diese Bewegungsfreiheit eine außergewöhnliche Gelassenheit hervorbringt, eine allumfassende Eindringlichkeit, aus der eine einladende Ausgewogenheit entsteht. Beim Betrachten der Bilder habe ich das Gefühl, eine Landkarte vor mir zu haben, und ich kann mir vorstellen, wie es wohl gewesen sein mag, als Kartografin das unbekannte Territorium ihrer Entstehung zu erkunden. Auf ihren Erkundungstouren lässt Rebecca Morris eine Form auf die nächste folgen, eine Farbe findet ihre Antwort in einer anderen Farbe, eine Handbewegung hebt die andere auf. Es entstehen Topografien nach dem Beispiel der Karte im Maßstab 1:1 in der berühmten Geschichte *Von der Strenge der Wissenschaft* von Jorge Luis Borges. Wie die Karte von Borges sind auch Morris' Gemälde Landschaft und deren Karte gleichermaßen.

Das Wissen, dass sie für das, was sie mit einem Gemälde ausdrücken möchte, die Freiheit in der Bewegung braucht, half mir, neu darüber nachzudenken, wie ich ihre Arbeit erlebe. Der Anblick der auf dem Boden ausgelegten Bilder erinnerte mich außerdem an Jackson Pollock. Dies ist natürlich irritierend, doch es drängt sich mir auf: Ich denke an Hans Namuths Schwarz-Weiß-Fotografien von Jackson Pollock aus dem Jahr 1950, wie er in seinem Atelier über seinen riesigen Leinwänden steht und die Farbe mit ausladenden Armbewegungen in dramatischen Bögen auf die Oberfläche tropfen und fließen lässt. Sobald ich einmal mit Pollock angefangen habe, wandern meine Gedanken weiter durch ein Dickicht aus kunsthistorischen Zusammenhängen und Meilensteinen in der Entwicklung der abstrakten Malerei und ich sinne nach über den Diskurs, welcher der zeitgenössischen

Kunst zugrunde liegt. Eine Wegscheide auf meiner inneren Reise sieht in etwa so aus: Ich denke an Jackson Pollock und dann an Lee Krasner, und wenn ich an sie denke, denke ich automatisch auch an Malerinnen im Allgemeinen und das Problem der Subjektivität. Ich denke an Lee Krasner und dann an den abstrakten Expressionismus als Ganzes und daran, wie Frauen aus der Diskussion über ihn ausgeschlossen sind. Diese ungeheuerliche Unterlassung beschwört wiederum das Bild von Helen Frankenthaler herauf, wie sie für ihr Interview in dem ansonsten wunderbaren Film *Painters Painting: The New York Art Scene, 1940–1970* aus dem Jahr 1973 in einer leeren Ecke platziert wurde, und diese eigenartige Ecke führt mich wiederum zu Carolee Schneemann und ihrem Werk *Up to and Including Her Limits*, 1973–76. Dort wird eine Ecke in den Dienst der Kunst gestellt, eine Malerin wird zur Mittlerin und ihr Schweben im Raum wird zur ästhetischen, weitschweifigen Geste.

Für *Up to and Including Her Limits* zog sich Carolee Schneemann in einem Gurt, der durch ein Seil an einem Flaschenzugsystem befestigt war, selbst hoch in die Luft und ließ sich wieder herab, sie schwang ihren Körper in jeden Winkel einer Zimmerecke und malte so auf große Papierbögen, die an den Wänden und auf dem Boden befestigt waren. Das Werk ist eine Landkarte des physischen Raumes, der durch den Körper der Künstlerin definiert wird. Es dokumentiert, wie sie ihre körperlichen und mentalen Grenzen auslotet, und beschreibt, wie sie ihre Flexibilität, ihre Ausdauer und ihr Durchhaltevermögen testet. Carolee Schneemann ist ausgebildete Malerin; *Up to and Including Her Limits* steht für sie in direktem Zusammenhang mit Pollocks „körperbetontem Malprozess“. „Mein gesamter Körper wird zum Mittler visueller Spuren, Relikte der Energie eines Körpers in Bewegung.“ (1) Mit diesem Werk hat sich Carolee Schneemann auf ein Abenteuer eingelassen und sich auf die Suche nach ihren Grenzen begeben. *Up to and Including Her Limits* beschreibt nicht nur die physische Reichweite ihres Körpers und ihr emotionales Vermögen, sondern steckt auch ein Gebiet ab. Sie setzt ein Zeichen und behauptet ihre Rolle als Malerin.

Schneemanns Nacktheit und die Präsenz ihres Körpers sowohl in den Performances als auch in der endgültigen Installation stellen eine direkte Konfrontation mit dem Platz der Frauen in der Geschichte der Malerei dar. Geschichten von Malern und ihren weiblichen Musen sind in der Kunstgeschichte weit verbreitet, Malerinnen hingegen müssen sich mit Fragen der Artikulation und der Repräsentation auseinandersetzen. *Up to and Including Her Limits* veranschaulicht dieses Dilemma und illustriert die begrenzte Freiheit der Malerin in den Weiten des männerdominierten abstrakten Expressionismus. Und doch gleicht Schneemanns Werk im Kern eher den Happenings von Allan Kaprow, die in ihren Anfängen ebenfalls eine direkte Antwort auf Pollock und das Versprechen eines performativen Raums der Malerei waren. Ihre Arbeit „hatte nichts mit Selbstoffenbarung oder Selbstdarstellung zu tun und sollte auch keine persönliche Geschichte erzählen. Es ging vielmehr um eine malerische Wahrnehmung der Umwelt als Raum für Collagen. *Up to and Including Her Limits* befindet sich tatsächlich im Dialog mit Jackson Pollock und der Bejahung des ganzen Körpers als Strich und Geste in diesem dimensionalen Raum.“ (2)

Wir sind also wieder bei Pollock. Allein, jetzt existiert eine zusätzliche Dimension der direkten Anrede. Mit *Up to and Including Her Limits* schuf Carolee Schneemann einen diskursiven Raum, in dem formelle Erkundungen stattfinden konnten; der Akt des Malens ist Teil der Kunst und die Rolle des Betrachters wird anerkannt. Schneemann tauchte in ihr Werk ein, sie markierte den Raum von innen und bewegte sich nach außen in Richtung seiner Grenzen. Rebecca Morris arbeitet um ihre Bildträger herum und über sie hinweg, sie nähert sich der Leinwand von außen. Dennoch ist die Frage der Körperlichkeit auch hier entscheidend: Morris' Arbeiten sähen anders aus, könnte sie ihre Bilder nicht von allen Seiten bearbeiten. In der endgültigen Installation von *Up to and Including Her Limits* ist Schneemann nicht mehr physisch präsent, doch die Anwesenheit ihres Körpers steht deutlich im Raum: Der leere Gurt hängt von der Decke, das Papier an den Wänden und auf dem Boden trägt ihre Handschrift, und auf den Monitoren zu beiden Seiten der Installation sind Videos von ihr zu sehen, die sie während der Performance zeigen. Gleichermaßen ist auch Rebecca Morris, wenn auch nicht physisch anwesend, durch die Spuren ihrer Handschrift und ihrer Herangehensweise präsent.

Während des Besuchs in ihrem Atelier, den ich eingangs erwähnte, zeigte sie mir ein Aquarell mit zinnoberroten Strichen auf burgunderrotem Grund. Die sechs Linien darauf sind so angeordnet, dass sie das Wort „HI" ergeben. Wie so viele ihrer Zeichnungen mit Text zeugt auch diese Arbeit von Charme und Witz. Es ist ein lockeres Bild, scheinbar aus der Hüfte geschossen – „Ich wollte nur mal eben ‚Hi' sagen!" – und es ist klug, stellt es doch die Bedeutung, die eine bestimmte Anordnung von Zeichen auf Papier erhalten kann, deutlich sichtbar unter Beweis. Und zu guter Letzt ist es auch noch optisch sehr ansprechend: Die Rottöne sind derart verführerisch und die Handbewegungen derart souverän, dass es plötzlich fast peinlich anmutet, ein Wort darin zu erkennen. Ich bin ganz und gar verzaubert von diesem flammenden, anmutigen Grußwort. Werde ich etwa rot?

Die Werke in Rebecca Morris' Ausstellung *Southafternoon* sind nicht weniger verblüffend in ihrer Offenheit. Die Gemälde sind entwaffnend und gleichermaßen selbstbewußt. Sie sind stark, mysteriös und auf sonderbare Weise schön. Ihr hervorstechendstes Merkmal jedoch ist ihre Offenheit, ihre Freundlichkeit: Hi. Wie Morris' Zeichnungen mit großen Initialen – die Signatur, die sich üblicherweise in der unteren rechten Ecke des Bildes befindet, wird so übertrieben vergrößert, dass sie vom Nachtrag zum Subjekt wird – gleicht auch dieses Grußwort einer persönlichen Einladung der Künstlerin an den Betrachter, mit ihr ins Gespräch zu kommen. Hi. Morris' Bilder halten uns nicht auf Abstand. Stattdessen behaupten sie sich als hochgradig originell, präsentieren sich als Ganzes und wenden sich direkt an uns. Sie aktivieren den in der Begegnung verborgenen Diskurs und erkennen so unsere Rolle als Betrachter an und bekunden die Tatsache ihrer Existenz; sie öffnen sich der Welt.

Als ich mich nach dem Titel der Ausstellung erkundigte, erzählte mir Rebecca Morris von dem Song *Southafternoon* auf *The Ann Steel Album* von Roberto Cacciapaglia aus dem Jahr 1979. Sie habe sich das Album und insbesondere diesen einen Song während der Arbeit an den Malereien für die Ausstellung immer wieder angehört und die Musik habe ihre Gemälde und ihre Stimmung zum Zeitpunkt ihrer Entstehung perfekt ergänzt. Ich hörte mir die Musik an und versuchte, einen Zusammenhang zu dem herzustellen, was ich in Morris' Gemälden sah, doch dann wurde mir klar, dass ich völlig auf dem Holzweg war. Rebecca Morris ist eine wahre Musikliebhaberin. Der Einfluss der Musik auf ihr Leben und ihre Arbeit ist gewaltig. Doch obschon die Musik sie gewiss beeinflusst und inspiriert, ist Musik nicht das *Thema* ihrer Arbeit.

Die zehn Elektropop-Songs auf *The Ann Steel Album* sind größtenteils unbeschwert und ohne Tempoänderung. Dadurch entsteht ein Gefühl unablässiger Vorwärtsbewegung, und da sich die Strophen, Refrains und Überleitungen vergleichsweise wenig voneinander unterscheiden, fühlen sich die Songs bisweilen wie eine Klangtapete an, deren Ästhetik vornehmlich auf großflächigen, symmetrischen Mustern gründet. Die Songs sind voll von Ecken und Kanten, die auf die eine oder andere Art abgerundet werden: Beats werden überzeichnet oder aufgelöst, langgezogene Töne verschmelzen mit Stakkati. Steels Stimme klingt oft gekünstelt oder irgendwie unnatürlich, eingestreute Klangeffekte pointieren ihre ungewöhnliche Darbietung, sie unterstreichen den synthetischen Charakter der Musik und führen dazu, dass der Überschwang ihrer Texte noch eine Nuance seltsamer anmutet.

Ich habe mir *The Ann Steel Album* so oft angehört, dass mir die Stücke nicht mehr aus dem Kopf gingen. Sie drifteten zwischen meinen Gedanken wie Wolken am blauen Himmel und mir wurde langsam klar, warum sich Rebecca Morris dieser Musik so verbunden fühlt. Ich konnte das weiße Licht Südkaliforniens in ihrem Studio regelrecht hören, ich konnte die Tonlagen der Musik vor meinem geistigen Auge sehen. Beim Anblick der Cover von Album und Single und beim Ansehen von

Steels Videoclip fielen mir die produktiven Gegensätze in der Musik und in der von ihr geschaffenen Rolle auf. Der Charakter „Ann Steel" ist eine Einzelgängerin, die sich frei durch außergewöhnliche Naturlandschaften bewegt, die mit futuristischen Stadtbildern verschmelzen. Sie ist wie eine Abenteurerin gekleidet: Ihre Kleidung ein funktioneller Overall mit Legionärskappe, an ihrem Gürtel hängt eine Wasserflasche und sie trägt Gamaschen und einen Rucksack. In dem Stück *Southafternoon* beschreibt Steel einen fiktiven tropischen Strand, an dem sie von der Terrasse eines Hotels aus auf eine der vielen surrealen Szenen blickt, in denen sie sich wiederfindet. „Green electric leaves / Many perfect palms / Small triangle sails slide on a chlorine blue sea / Artificial rainbows / Colours have their wavelength / Seagulls draw a diagram up high." (Grüne elektrische Blätter / Viele perfekte Palmen/ Kleine dreieckige Segel auf einem türkisblauen Meer / Künstliche Regenbogen / Farben haben ihre Wellenlänge / Möwen zeichnen etwas in den Himmel). Dieselbe Art von Tempo, von Bewegung, von selbstbewusstem Forscherdrang prägt auch Morris' neuere Gemälde. Sie ist eine furchtlose Reisende, die über die Freiheit, den Mut und das Wissen verfügt, ihre Grenzen auszuloten und zu überschreiten und sich dabei in einer von ihr selbst geschaffenen Landschaft bewegt, in der sich diese Grenzen unablässig, unumgänglich, verändern.

(1) Carolee Schneemann, Statement der Künstlerin
http://www.caroleeschneemann.com/uptoandincluding.html
(2) Behind the Scenes: On Line:
Carolee Schneemann, MoMA-Videos, 2010
https://www.youtube.com/watch?v=sm04OR3Gvq8

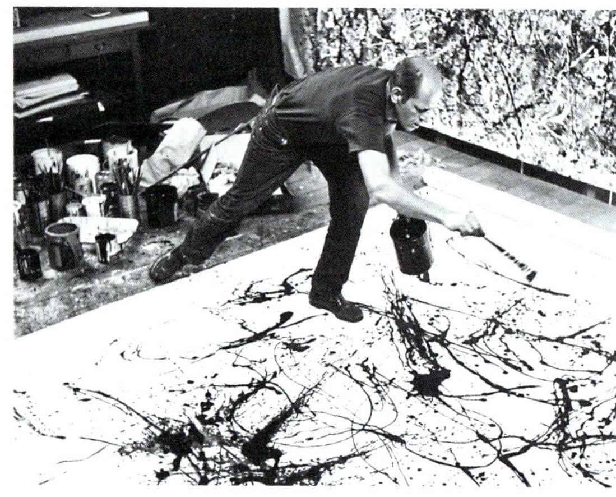

Jackson Pollock, 1950
Fotografie von / Photograph by Hans Namuth
Courtesy Center for Creative Photography, University of Arizona
© 1991 Hans Namuth Estate

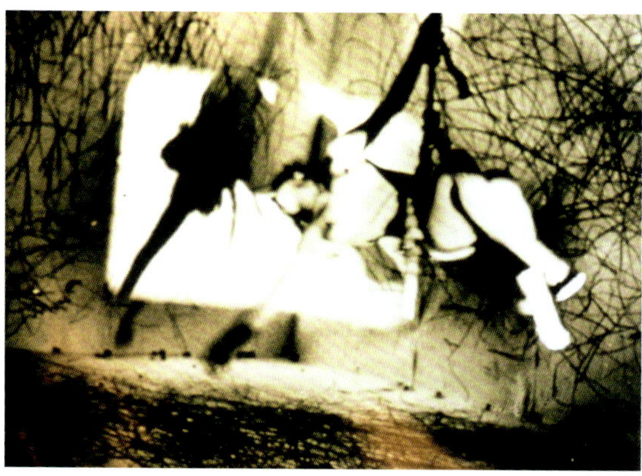

Carolee Schneemann, *Up to and Including Her Limits*, 1973–76
Performance: Buntstift auf Papier, Seil & an der Decke befestigter Gurt / Crayon on paper, rope & harness suspended from ceiling

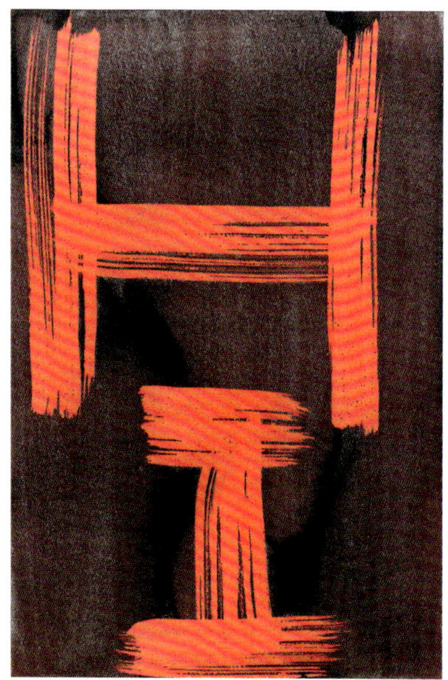

Rebecca Morris, *Untitled (#134-00)*, 2000
Aquarell und Tinte auf Papier / Watercolor and ink on paper 38 × 25 cm / 14¾ × 10 in
Sammlung / Collection Mac McCaughan & Andrea Reusing

Corrina Peipon

Hi.

I recently went to Rebecca Morris's studio with the intention of getting a better idea of what it is like for her to make her paintings. I wanted to try to reconcile my own sense of what her paintings are from the standpoint of a viewer with what it is that she sees, what she is going for, and how she makes her work. When I arrived, Morris asked me to give her a hand. Together, we moved one painting from a prone to an upright position and then retreated to look at all of her new paintings leaning up against the walls. The floor, as it usually is, was littered with protective coverings, tape, and paper bowls filled with mixed paint and brushes. She told me not to worry about stepping on anything. I looked down at my feet and the bowls of pigment strewn all across the floor, and I saw the negative space where the painting we'd just moved had been lying out prior to my arrival. When I looked back at the paintings, they all of a sudden went topsy-turvy, and I felt as though I was finally able to *see* something I'd been looking at for a very long time.

Morris works almost exclusively on the floor, laying out paper or canvas drop cloths that sometimes become the foundation for new paintings, in turn. She lays out her stretched canvases atop the tarps and goes to town. Looking down on the painting she is working on, Morris can move around the canvas at will, adding gestures from any side, angle, direction. In this way, there is no top or bottom, left or right; she is unimpeded by prescribed directionality. The paintings are like aerial views of their own making or a compass plate on which magnetic north is always changing. My sense of it is that, as a result of this freedom of movement, there is an unusual equanimity, an all-over emphasis that yields a welcoming balance. When I look at these paintings, I feel like I am looking at a map, and I can imagine what it must have been like to be the cartographer on an expedition into the unknown territory of its making. Moving from one shape to another, responding to one color with another color, using one gesture to offset the last, the paintings are the result of Morris's wayfinding. The results are topographies that read like the map drawn at a scale of one to one in Jorge Luis Borges's famous story *On Exactitude in Science*. Like Borges's map, Morris's painting is at once terrain and map thereof.

The notion of freedom of movement as a requirement for achieving the results she is going for in a painting helped me to think in a new way about how I experience Morris's work. Seeing the work laid out on the floor also made me think of Jackson Pollock. This, of course, is distracting, but I can't help it: I think of Hans Namuth's black and white photographs of Jackson Pollock in his studio in 1950, bending over his enormous canvases and reaching out to drip and drab the paint in dramatic arcs across their surfaces. Once I start in on Pollock, my mind wanders through a tangle of art historical lineages and milestones in the development of abstract painting and the discourse that is foundational to contemporary art. One forking path on my mental journey goes somewhere like this: I think of Pollock and then Lee Krasner, and when I think of Krasner, I think of female painters and the conundrum of subjectivity. I think of Krasner and then abstract expressionism as a whole and the exclusion of women in the discussion of it. This egregious omission conjures the image of Helen Frankenthaler shoved into a blank corner for her interview in the otherwise wonderful 1973 film *Painters Painting: The New York Art Scene, 1940–1970*, and that awkward corner brings me to Carolee Schneemann and her work *Up to and Including Her Limits,* 1973–76, a piece in which a corner is put to work in service of art, a female painter asserts agency, and her act of navigating space becomes an aesthetic, discursive gesture.

For *Up to and Including Her Limits,* Carolee Schneemann used a pulley system attached to a harness to lift herself up and down and swing her body into the far reaches of a corner of a room to draw on large sheets of paper attached to the intersecting walls and floor. The work is a map of the physical space defined by Schneemann's body. It is documentation of Schneemann approaching and describing her physical and mental limits, testing her flexibility, endurance, and mettle. Trained as a painter, Schneemann describes *Up to and Including Her Limits* as being in conversation with Pollock's "physicalized painting process." "My entire body becomes the agency of visual traces, vestiges of the body's energy in motion."(1) In making this work, Schneemann embarked on an adventure to seek out her edges. *Up to and Including Her Limits* not only describes the physical reach of Schneemann's body and her emotional acumen but marks out a territory. She stakes her claim and declares her agency as a painter.

The fact of Schneemann's nudity and the presence of her body in both the performances and in the final installation is a direct confrontation of the place of women in the history of painting. Much of art history tells the story of male painters and female subjects, leaving female painters to ponder questions of agency and representation. *Up to and Including Her Limits* demonstrates this bind, literalizing the constrained freedom of the female painter in the far reaches of the male-dominated abstract expressionist field. Schneemann's work, though, is at its core more akin to Allan Kaprow's Happenings, the earliest of which were also a direct response to Pollock and the promise of the performative space of painting. Schneemann's work "had nothing to do with self-confession or self-exposure or personal narrative. It had to do with a painterly sense of the environment as a collage arena. *Up to and Including Her Limits* really is in discussion with Jackson Pollock and the allowance for the whole body as stroke and gesture in this dimensional space." (2)

And so, we are back to Pollock. But now there is an added dimension of direct address. With *Up to and Including Her Limits,* Schneemann set up a discursive space in which formal exploration could take place, the act of painting is part of the art, and the role of the viewer is acknowledged. Schneemann immersed herself in her work, marking the space from the inside and moving out toward its boundary. Morris works around and across her surfaces, approaching the canvas from the outside. Still, the question of physicality is crucial: Morris's paintings would not look the way they look if she could not approach the canvas from all directions. In the final iteration of *Up to and Including Her Limits,* Schneemann is not physically present, but the evidence of her body is explicit: an empty harness hangs from the ceiling, the paper on the walls and floor is filled with her marks, and the video monitors that flank the installation play footage showing Schneemann performing the work. Similarly, while not physically there, Morris is present through the evidence of her mark-making and her mode of address.

During the same visit to her studio that I mentioned earlier, Morris showed me a drawing made from strokes of vermillion pigment over a burgundy ground. Its six lines are oriented in such a way that they spell out the word "HI." The work, like many of her drawings that contain text, is charming and funny. It's casual, seemingly offhand—"Just dropped in to say 'hi'!"—and it's smart, making a visual argument for the significance that can be found in a particular arrangement of marks on paper. All that, and handsome, too: the shades of red are so seductive and the gestures are so assured that it's suddenly almost embarrassing to recognize them as a word. Entranced by this blazing, poised salutation, I wonder if I'm blushing ...

The works in Rebecca Morris's exhibition *South-afternoon* are similarly striking in their forthrightness. The paintings disarm even while being assertive. They are strong, mysterious, and oddly beautiful. But the clincher is that they are open and friendly: Hi. Like her drawings that feature her initials writ large—the customary lower right corner signature blown all out of proportion to the point at which they become more subject than afterthought—this greeting is like a personal invitation from the artist to the viewer to engage in a conversation. Hi. Morris's works do not hold us at arm's length. Instead, they assert themselves as highly individuated, present themselves as whole, and directly address us. They open up to the world by expressing the fact of their existence and recognizing our role as viewers in activating the discourse latent in the encounter.

When I asked about the title of the exhibition, Morris told me about Roberto Cacciapaglia, his 1979 release *The Ann Steel Album*, and the song *Southafternoon*. She told me that she listened to the album and especially that song over and over while she was making the works in the exhibition, that the music had been a perfect complement to her paintings and her disposition at the time of their making. I listened to the music, trying to find the kinship between it and what I saw in Morris's paintings, but then I realized I was getting it all wrong. Morris is a serious music fan. Its influence on her life and work can't be understated. But while she is certainly affected and inspired by music, her work is not *about* music.

The ten electro-pop songs on *The Ann Steel Album* are generally upbeat and absent of dynamics. This consistency of texture yields a feeling of unceasing forward motion, and since the verses, choruses, and bridges are comparatively indiscernible, the songs often feel like sonic wallpaper with symmetrical overall patterning as the dominant aesthetic strategy. The songs are filled with jagged edges that are smoothed over in one way or another: beats are stilted or arpeggiated, and elongated sounds elide with staccato notes. Steel's voice often sounds strained or vaguely unnatural, and occasional vocal effects play up her unusual delivery, underscoring the synthetic nature of the music and adding a layer of weirdness to the manufactured exuberance of her lyrics.

I listened to *The Ann Steel Album* enough that the songs began to inhabit my mind, drifting among my thoughts like clouds across a blue sky, and I started to recognize the affinity Morris may have found in the music. I could somehow hear the white southern California light in her studio and see the sonic layers of the music in my mind's eye. Looking at the album and single covers and watching performance video of Steel, I was struck by the productive contradictions at work in the music and in the persona she created. The character "Ann Steel" is a lone woman moving freely through extraordinary natural landscapes that merge with futuristic urban environments. She is dressed for adventure: her uniform is a utilitarian jumpsuit and legionnaire hat; a water bottle hangs from her belt; she wears protective gaiters and a backpack. In the song *Southafternoon*, Steel describes a science fiction tropical beach setting where she gazes out from a hotel patio at one of the many surreal scenes in which she finds herself: "Green electric leaves / Many perfect palms / Small triangle sails slide on a chlorine blue sea / Artificial rainbows / Colours have their wavelength / Seagulls draw a diagram up high." A similar kind of pacing, movement, and confident exploration is evident in Morris's recent paintings: she is an intrepid traveler with the freedom, guts, and know-how to reach up to and beyond her limits in a landscape of her own creation where said limits are always, necessarily changing.

(1) Carolee Schneemann, artist statement
http://www.caroleeschneemann.com/uptoandincluding.html
(2) Behind the Scenes: On Line:
Carolee Schneemann, MoMA-videos, 2010
https://www.youtube.com/watch?v=smo4OR3Gvq8

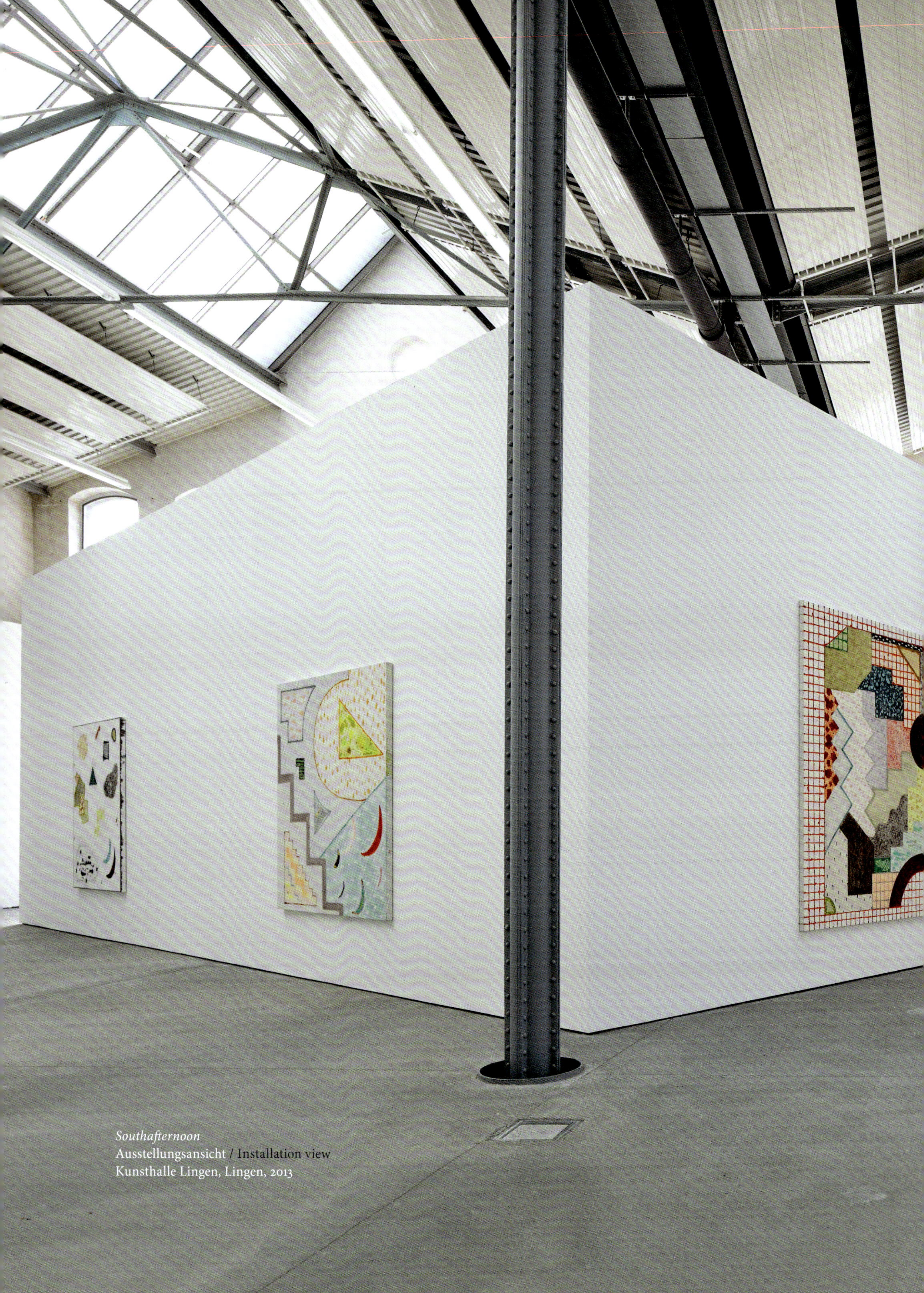

Southafternoon
Ausstellungsansicht / Installation view
Kunsthalle Lingen, Lingen, 2013

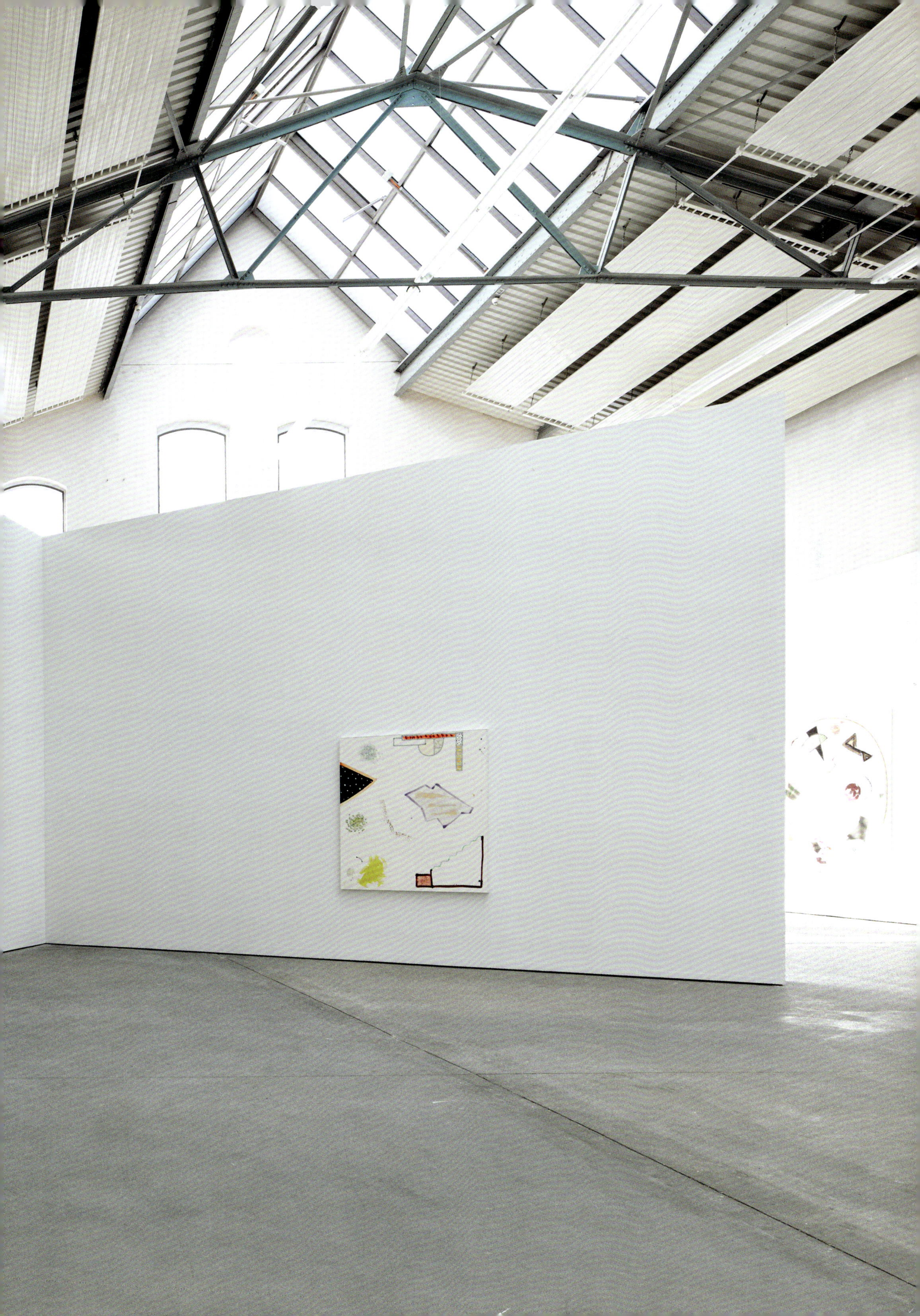

Untitled (#01-13), 2013
Öl auf Leinwand / Oil on canvas 221 × 203 cm / 87 × 80 in

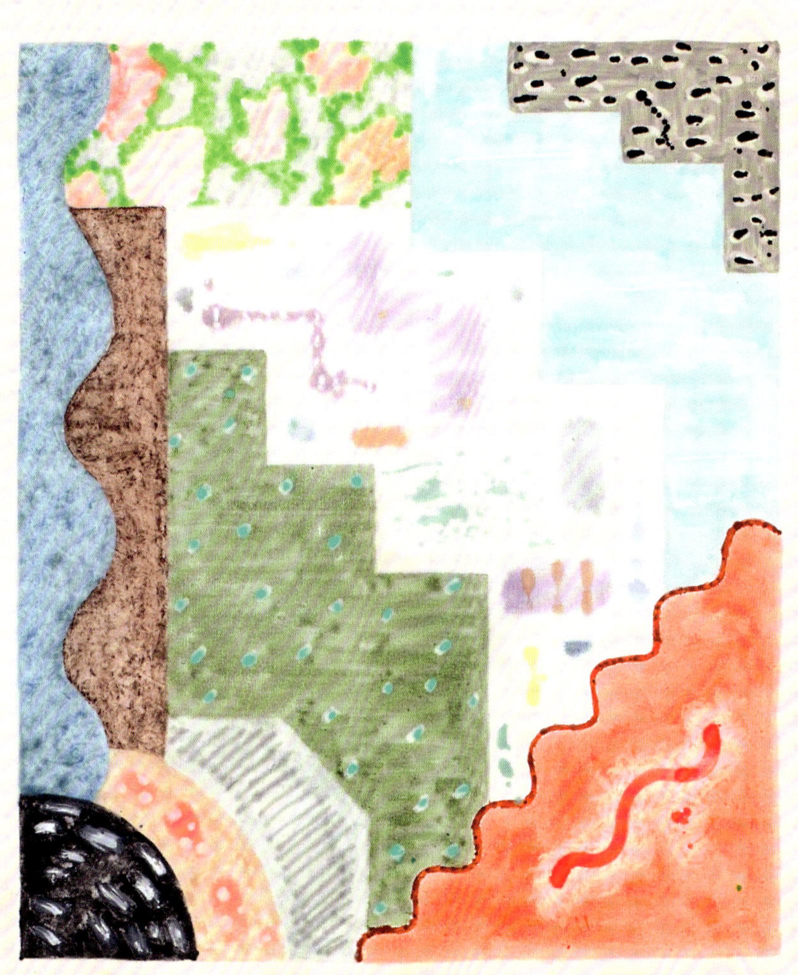

Untitled (#03-13), 2013
Öl auf Leinwand / Oil on canvas 178 × 178 cm / 70 × 70 in

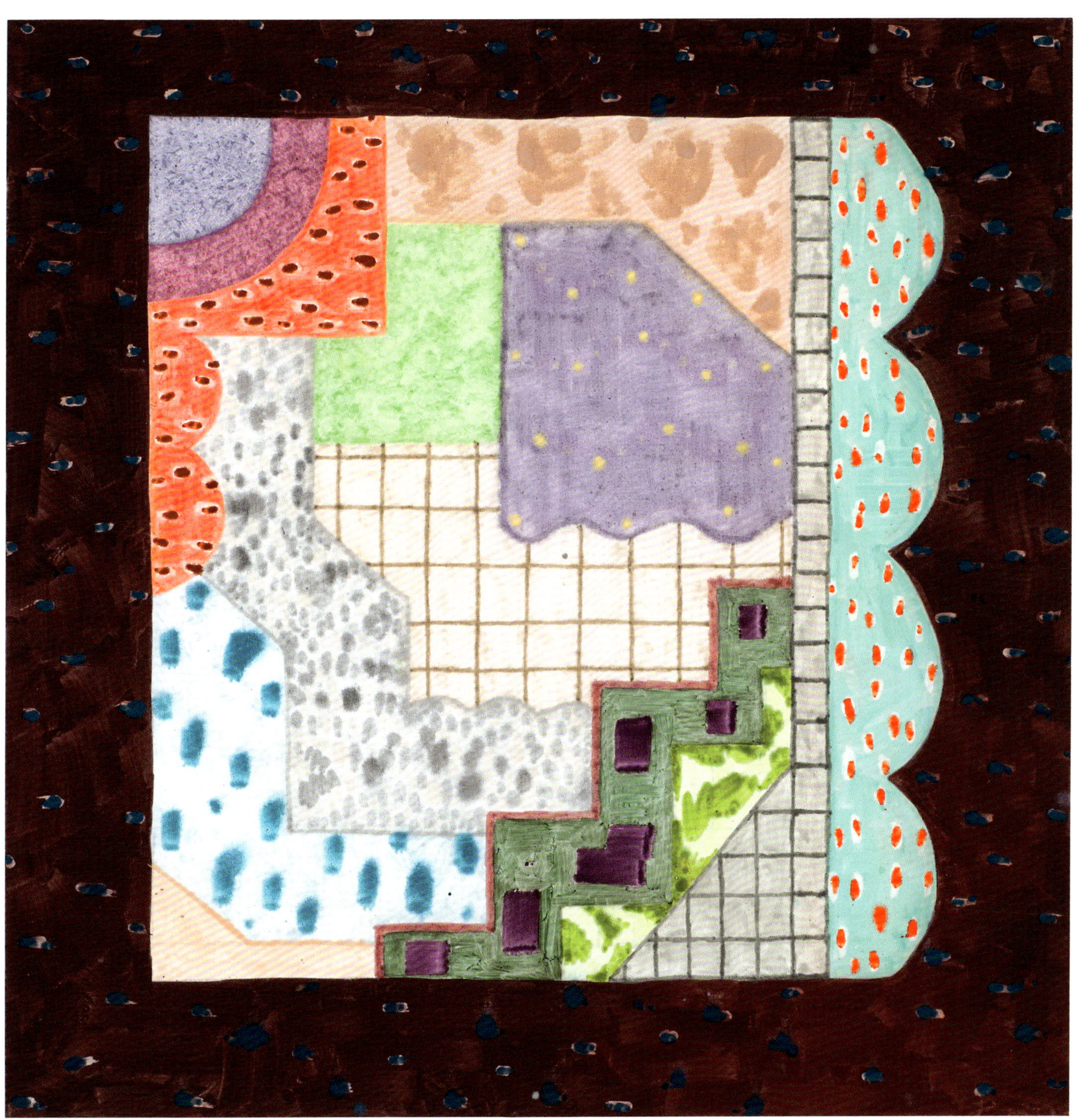

Untitled (#04-13), 2013
Öl auf Leinwand / Oil on canvas 147 × 147 cm / 58 × 58 in

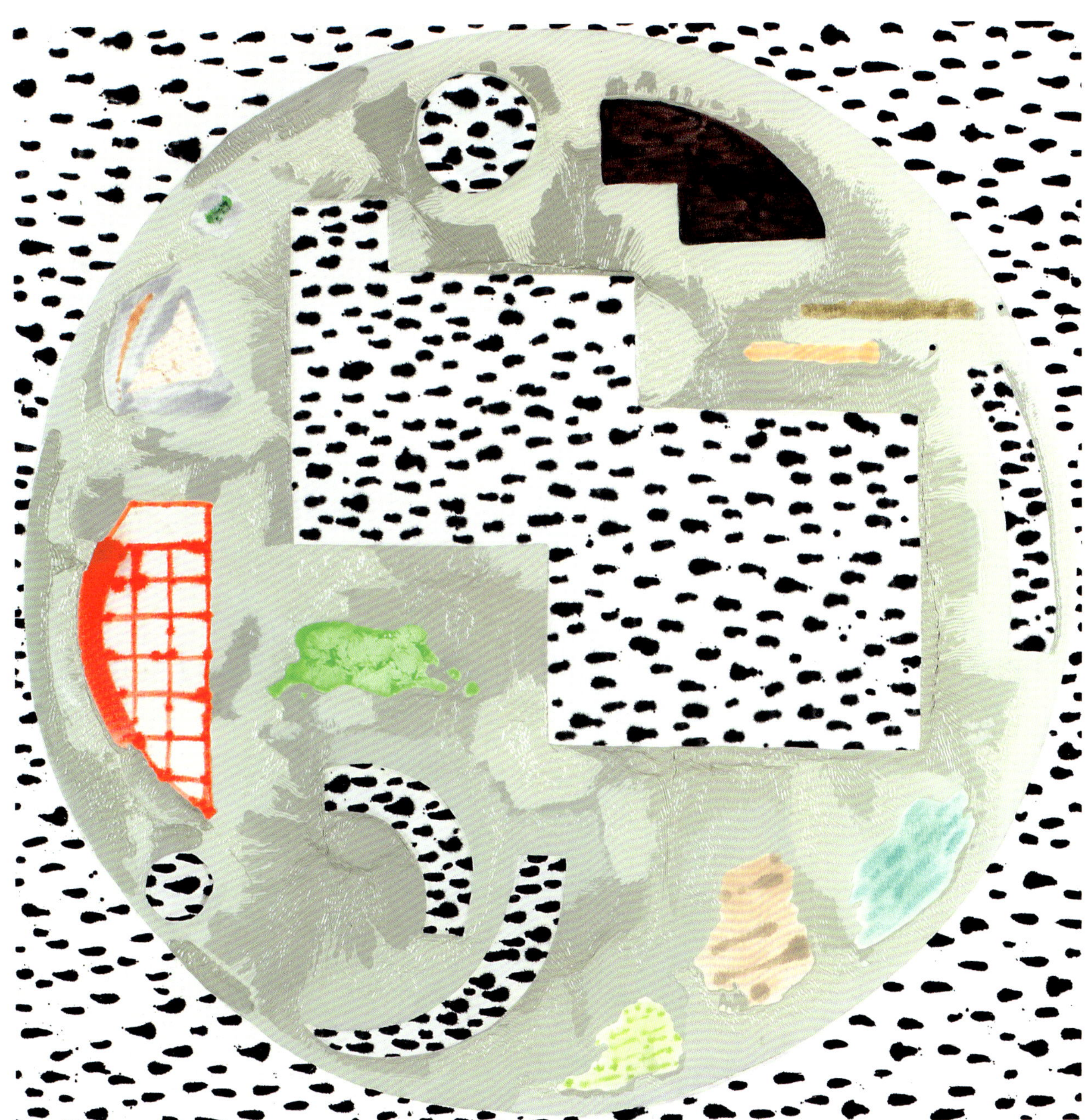

Untitled (#01-12), 2012
Öl auf Leinwand / Oil on canvas 203 × 175 cm / 80 × 69 in

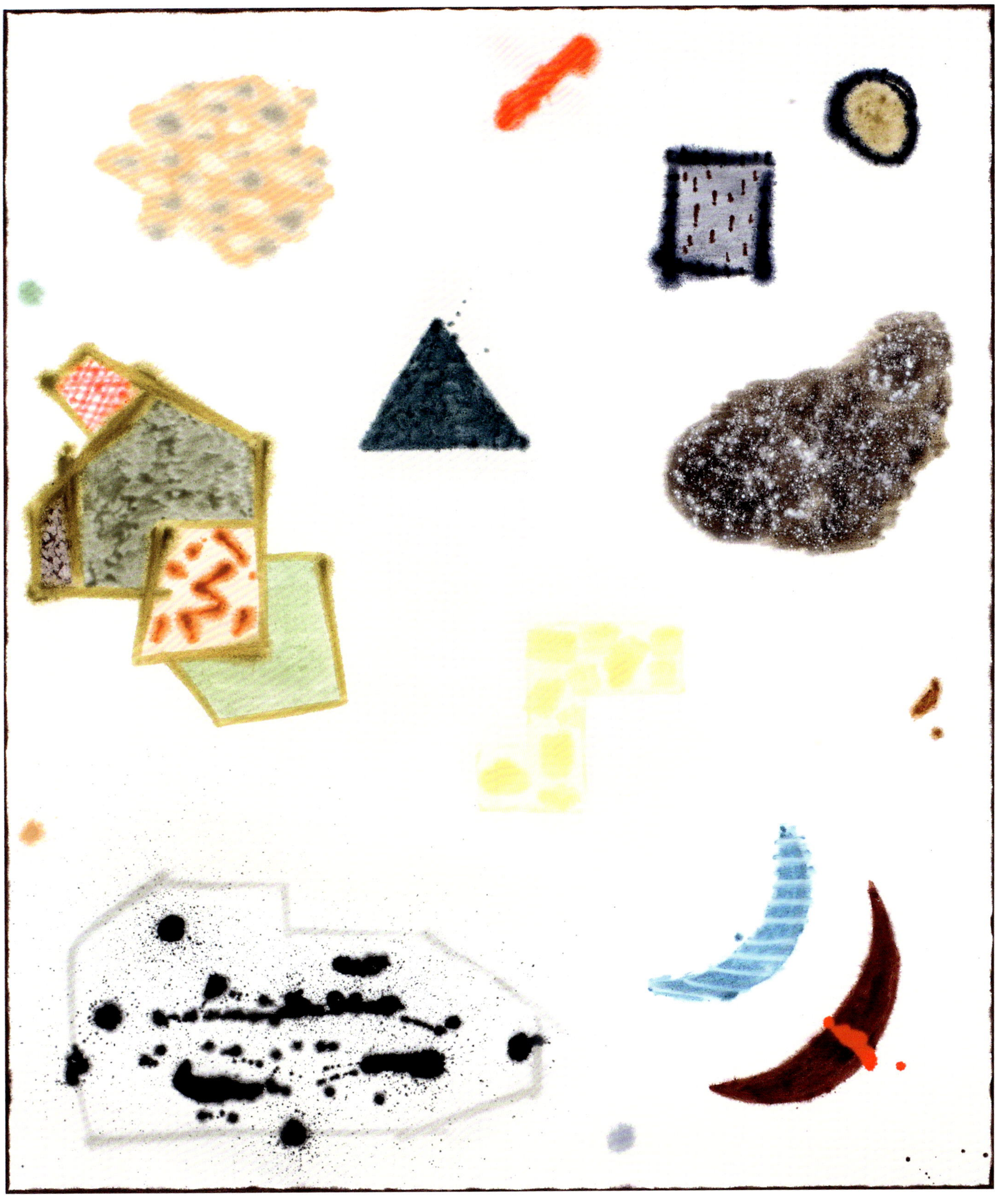

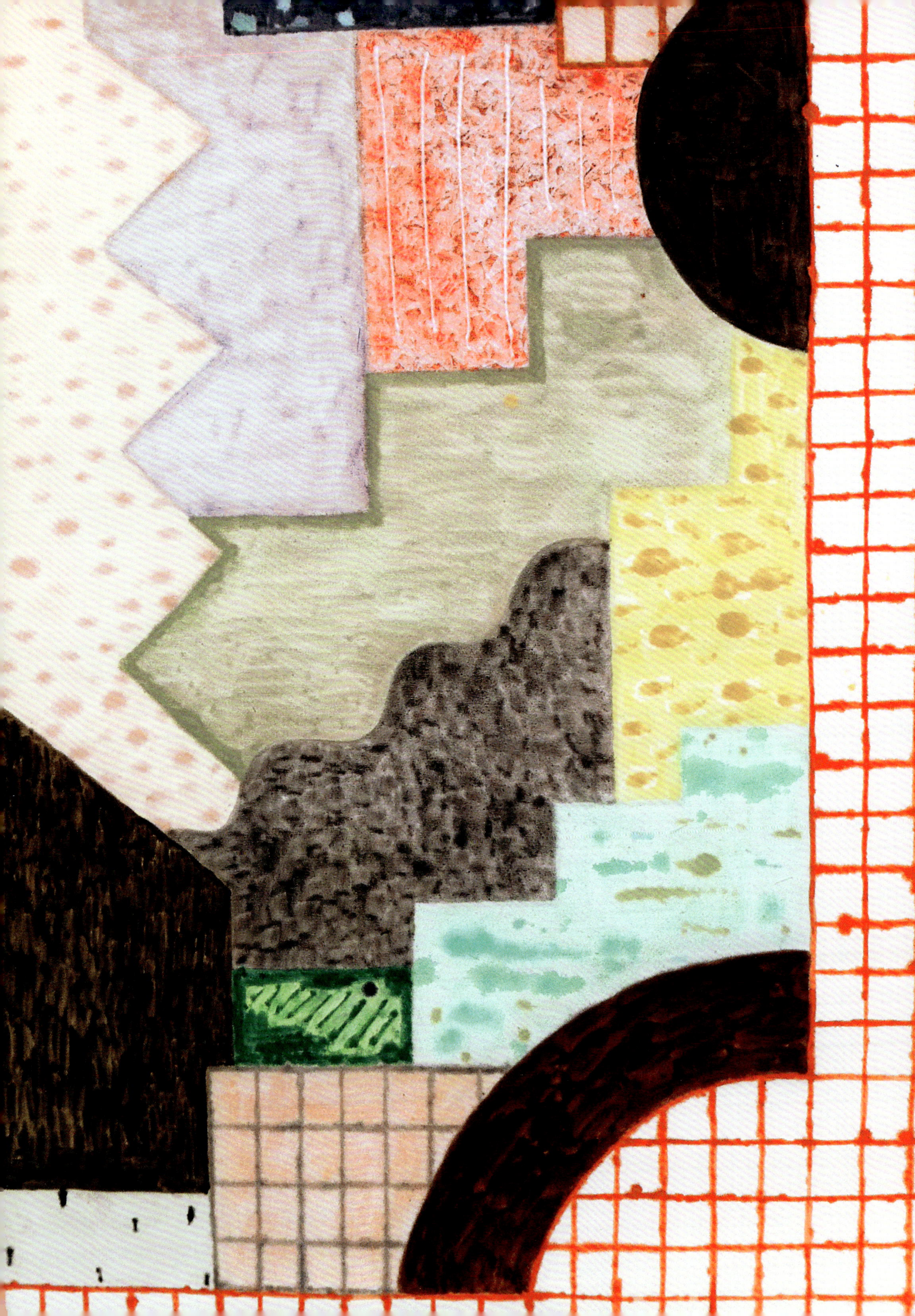

Untitled (#02-12), 2012
Öl auf Leinwand / Oil on canvas 269 × 205 cm / 106 × 80½ in

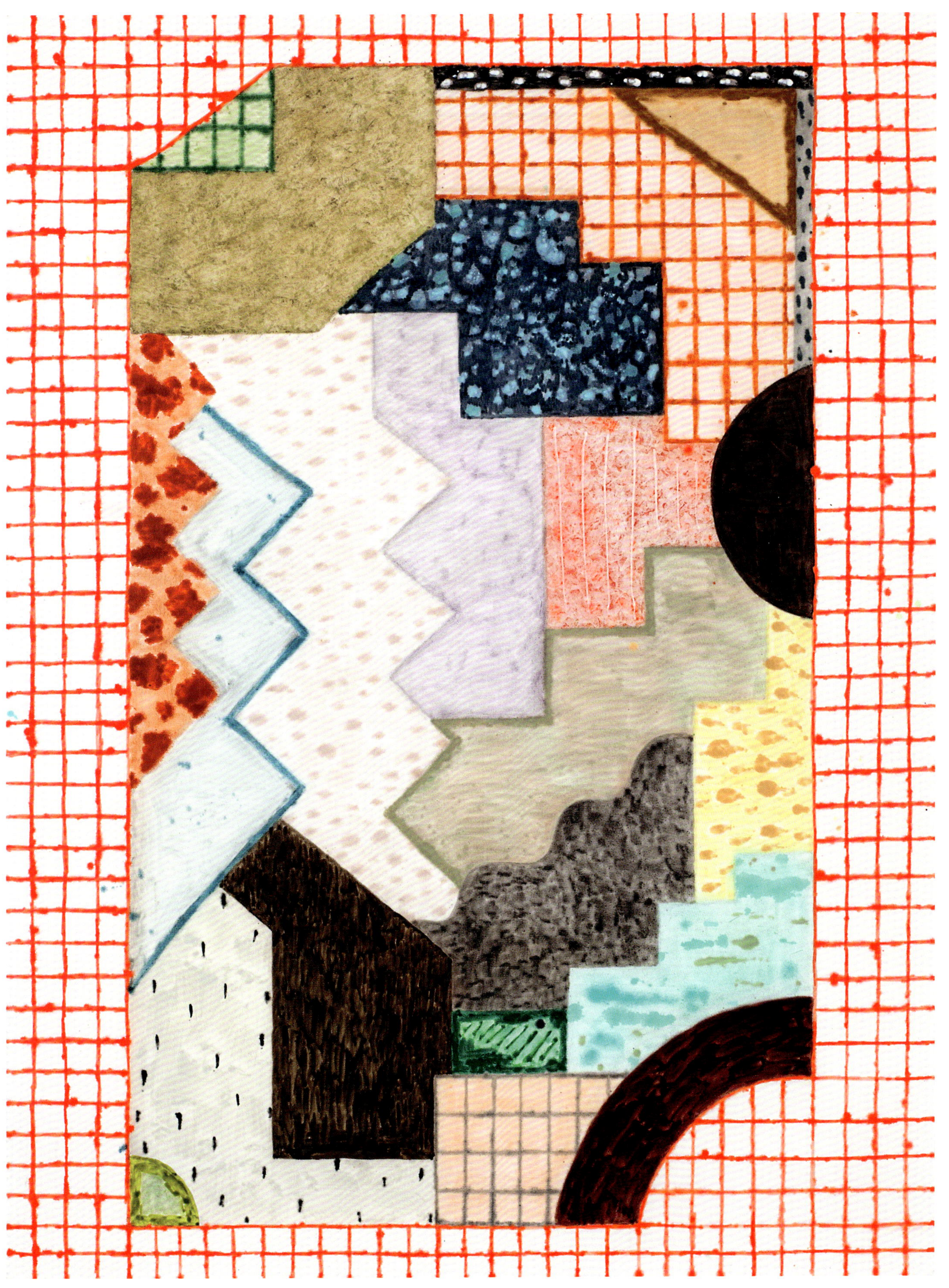

Untitled (#01-11), 2011
Öl auf Leinwand / Oil on canvas 107 × 107 cm / 42 × 42 in

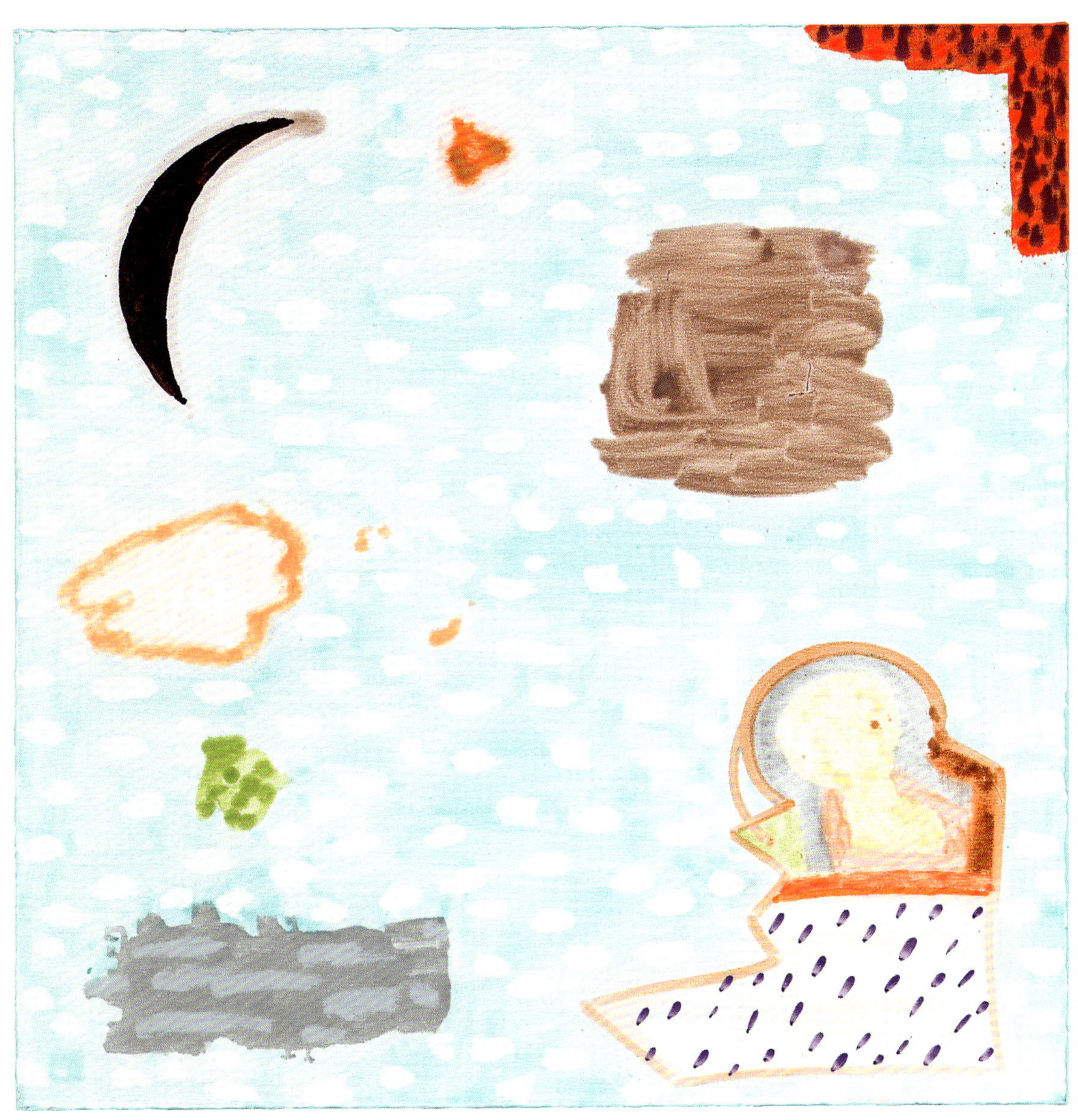

Untitled (#05-11), 2011
Öl und Sprühfarbe auf Leinwand / Oil and spray paint on canvas 218 × 198 cm / 85 ¾ × 78 in

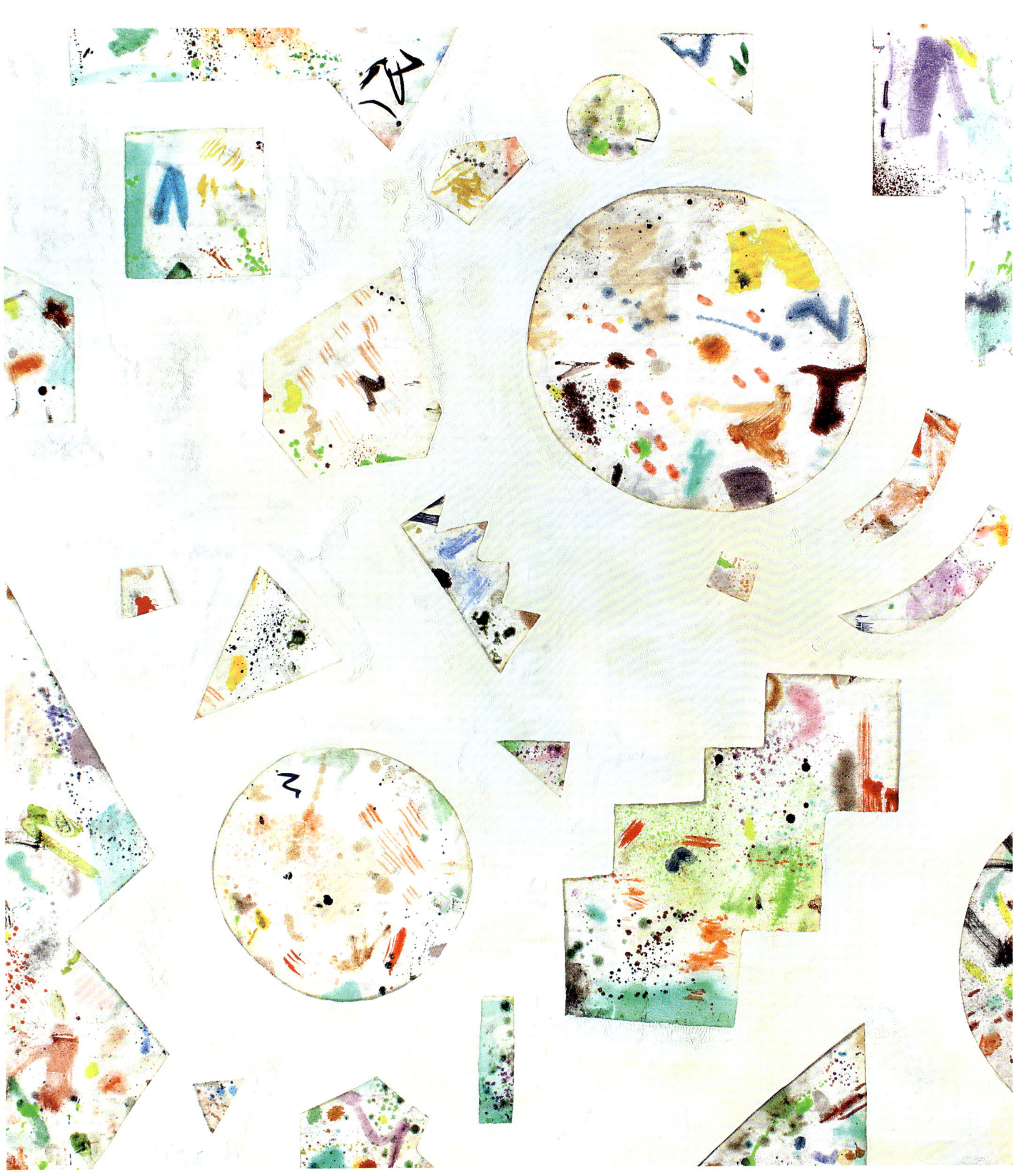

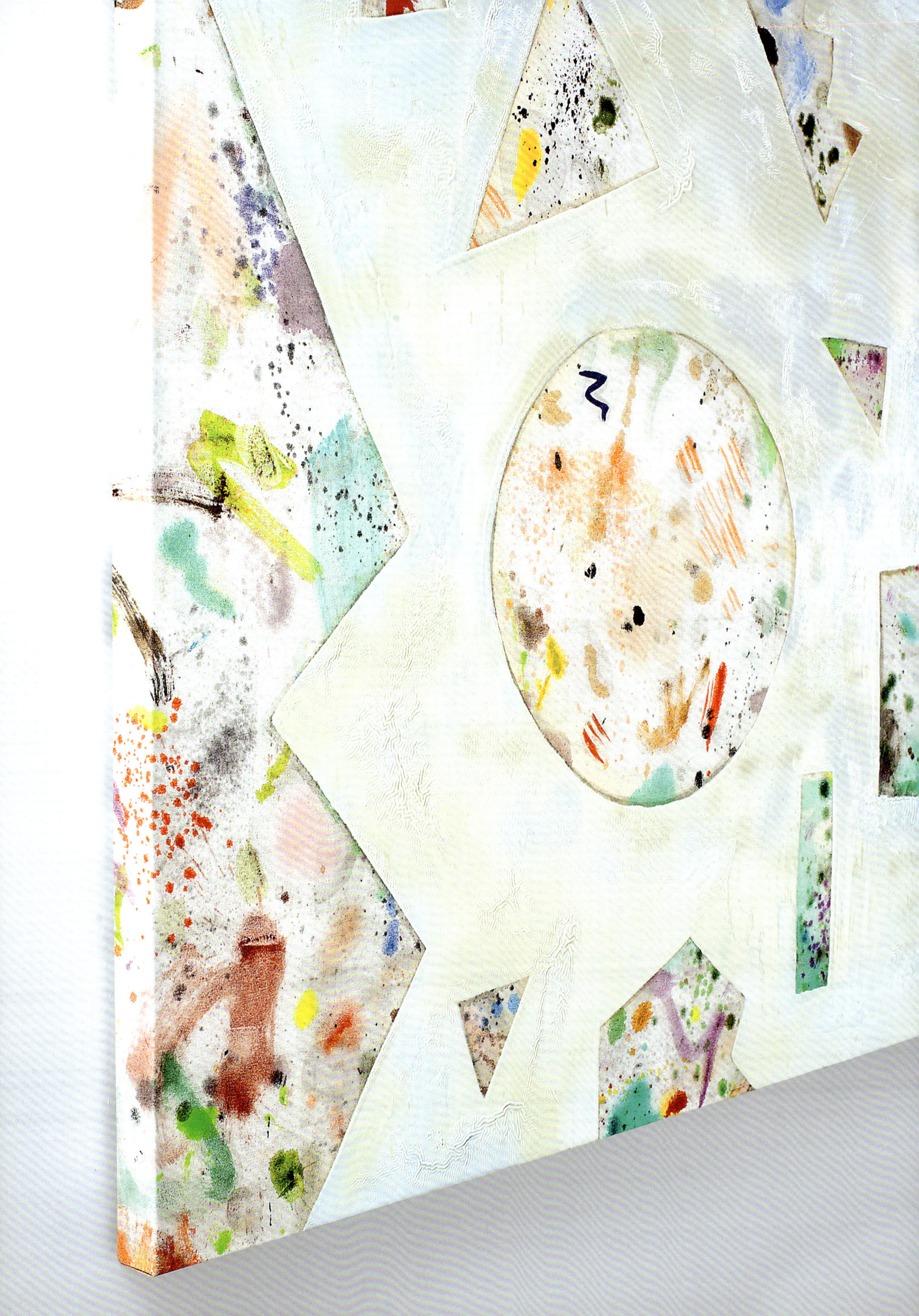

Untitled (#07-11), 2011
Öl auf Leinwand / Oil on canvas 203 × 207 cm / 80 × 81½ in

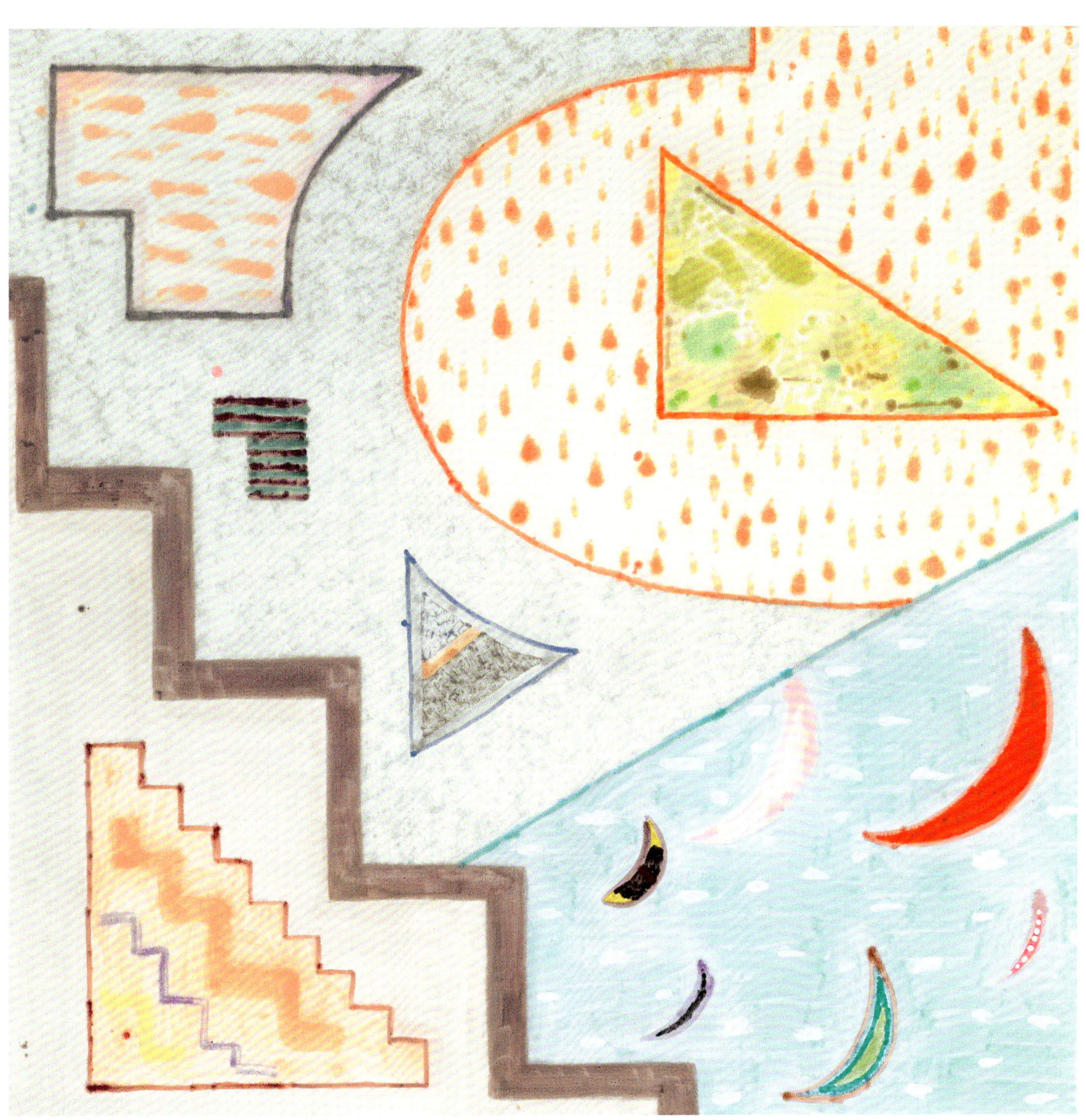

Untitled (#05-09), 2009
Öl und Sprühfarbe auf Leinwand / Oil and spray paint on canvas 165 × 165 cm / 65 × 65 in

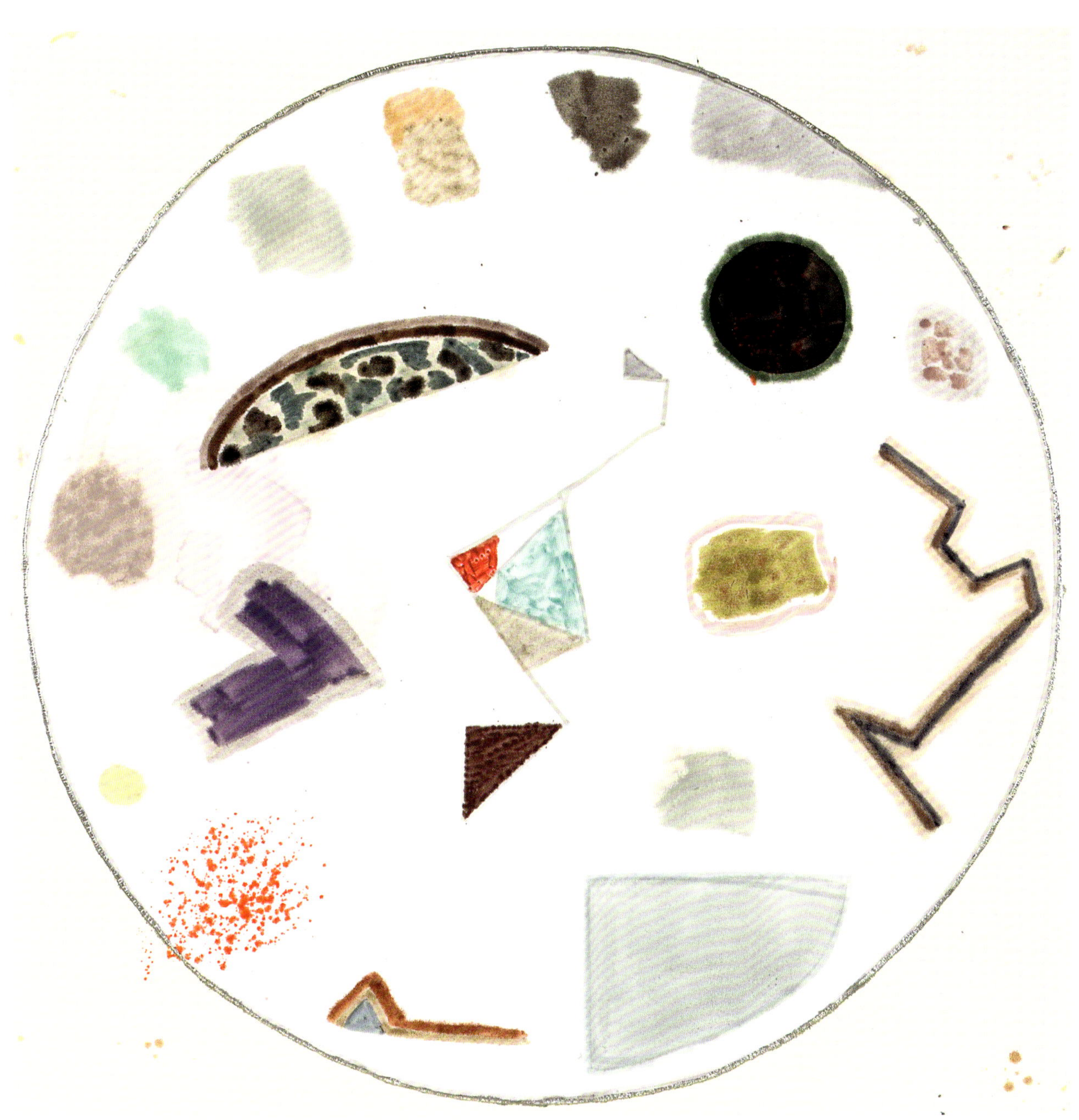

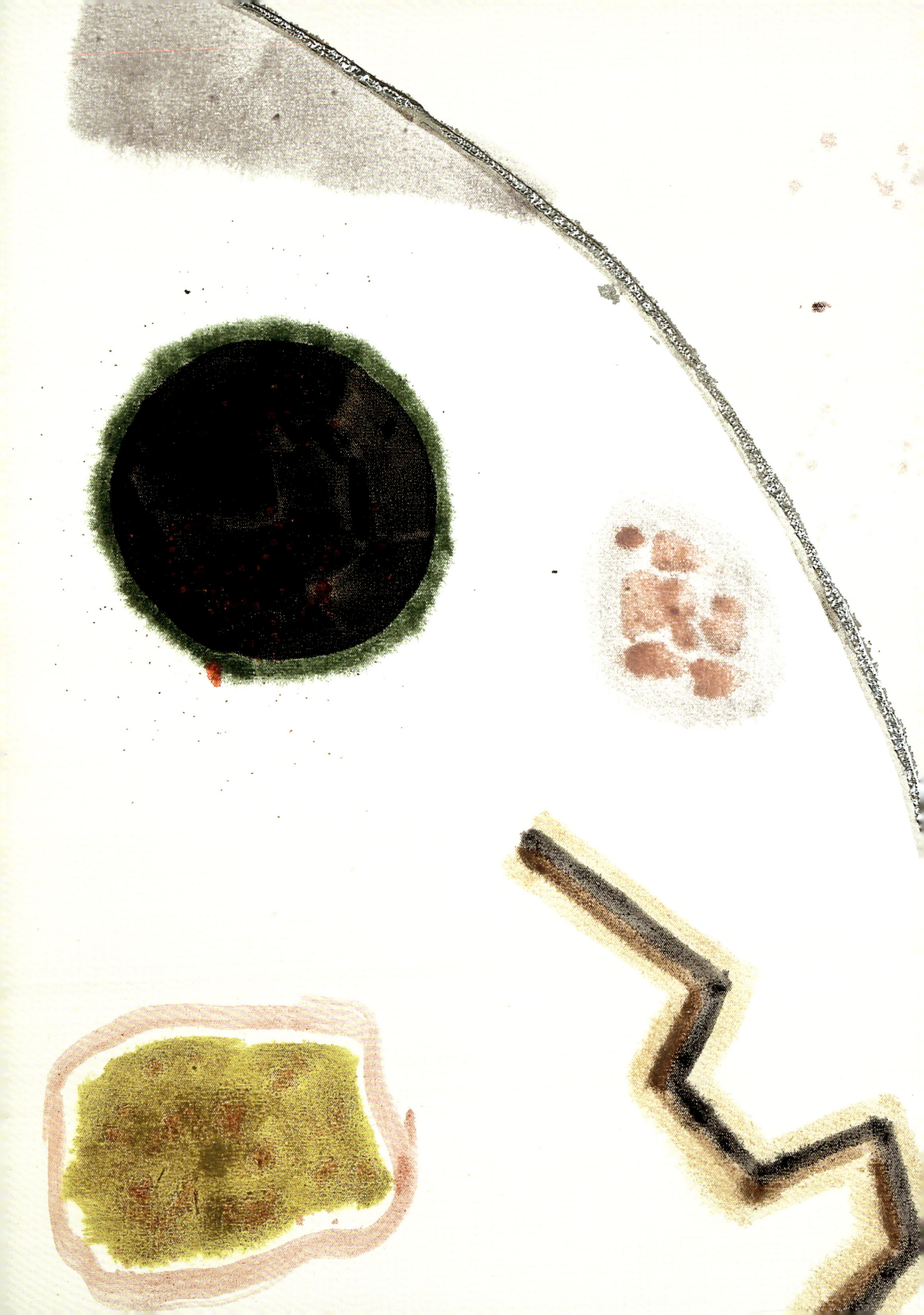

Untitled (#05-10), 2010
Öl auf Leinwand / Oil on canvas 152 × 149 cm / 60 × 58 ½ in

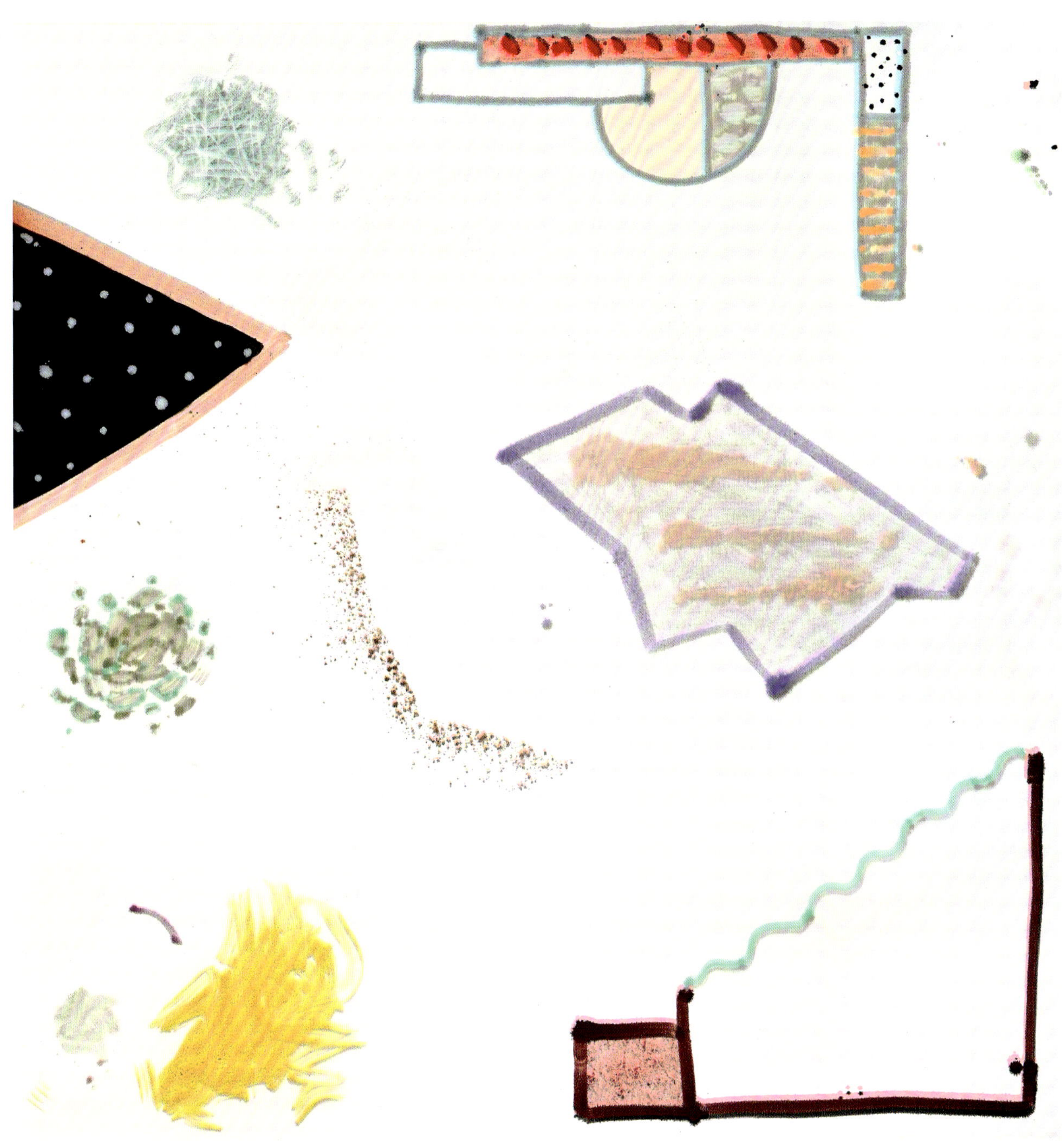

Untitled (#08-10), 2010
Öl auf Leinwand / Oil on canvas 149 × 153 cm / 58 ½ × 60 in

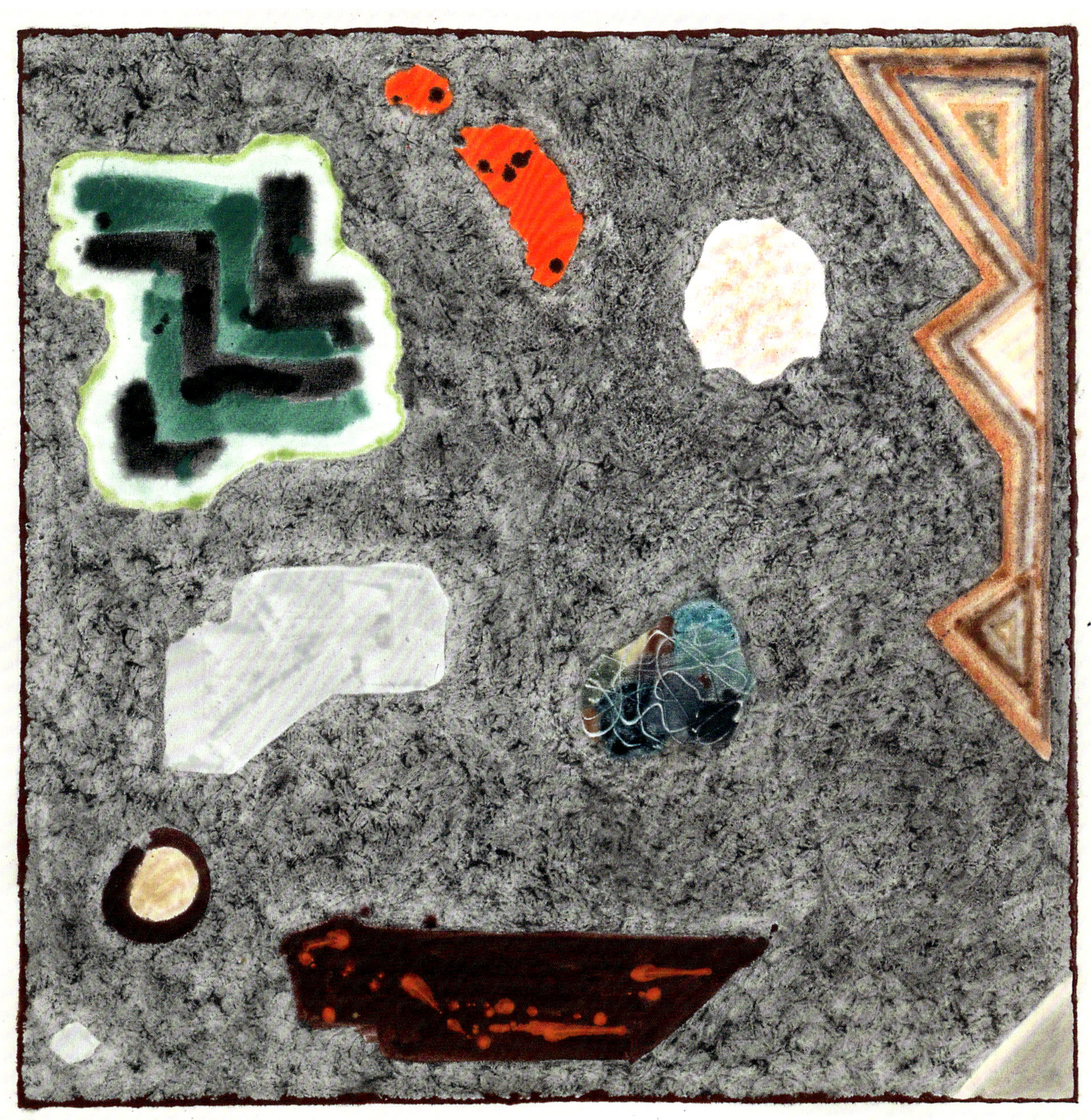

Untitled (#01-09), 2009
Öl und Sprühfarbe auf Leinwand / Oil and spray paint on canvas 229 × 193 cm / 90 × 76 in

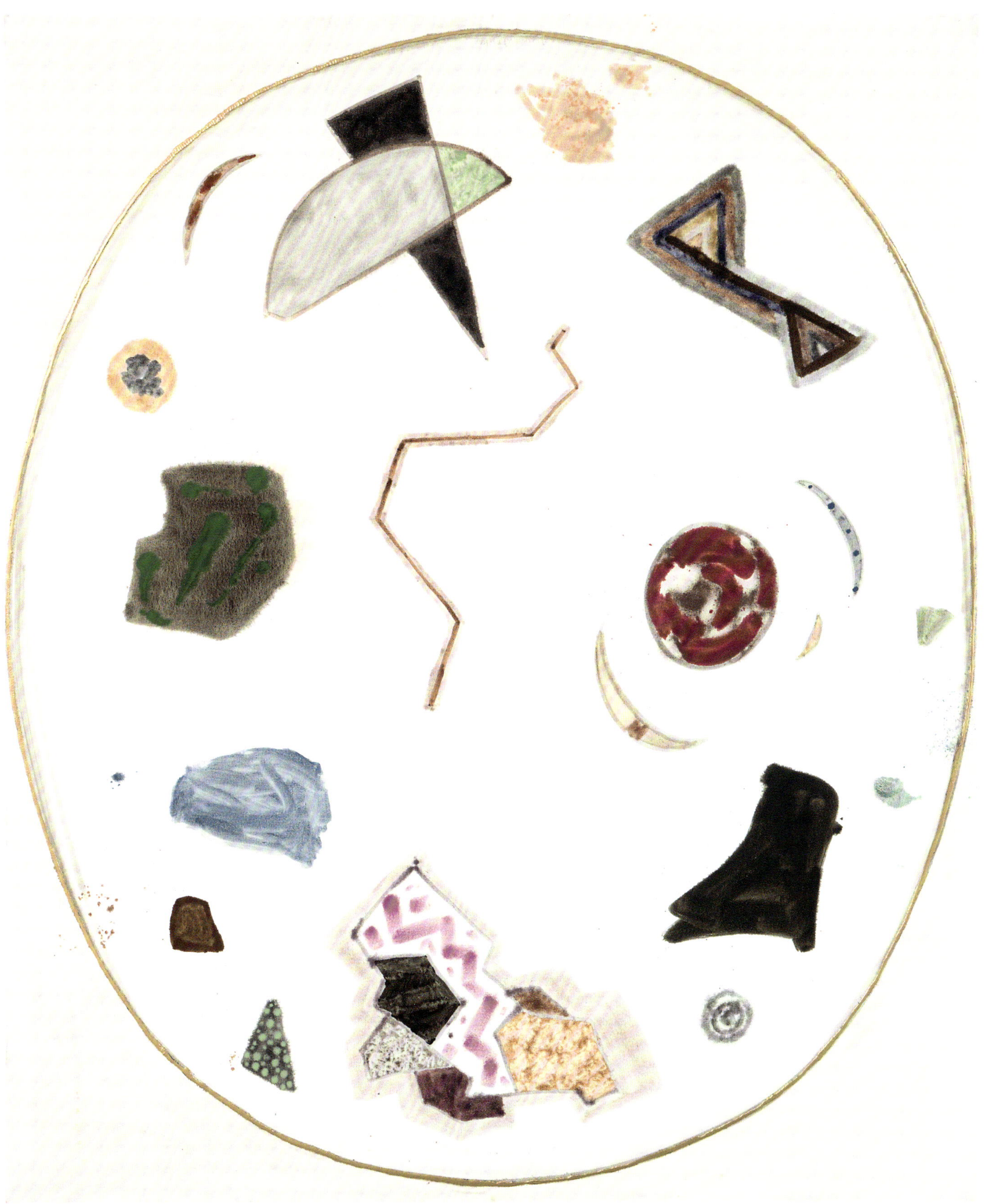

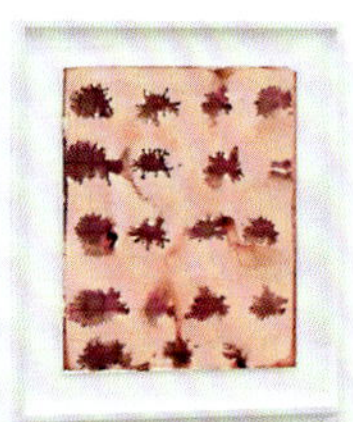
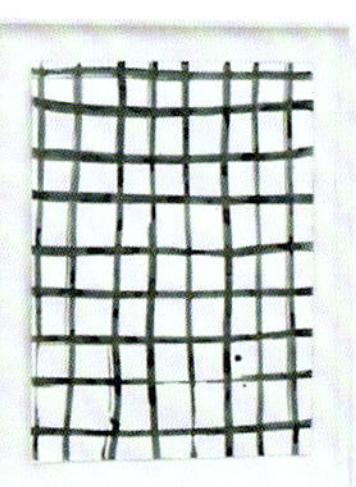
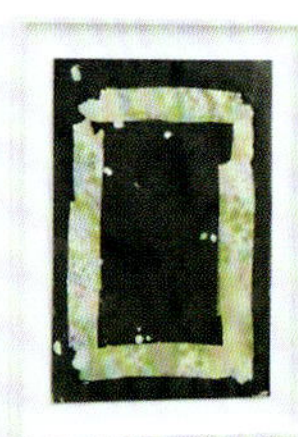

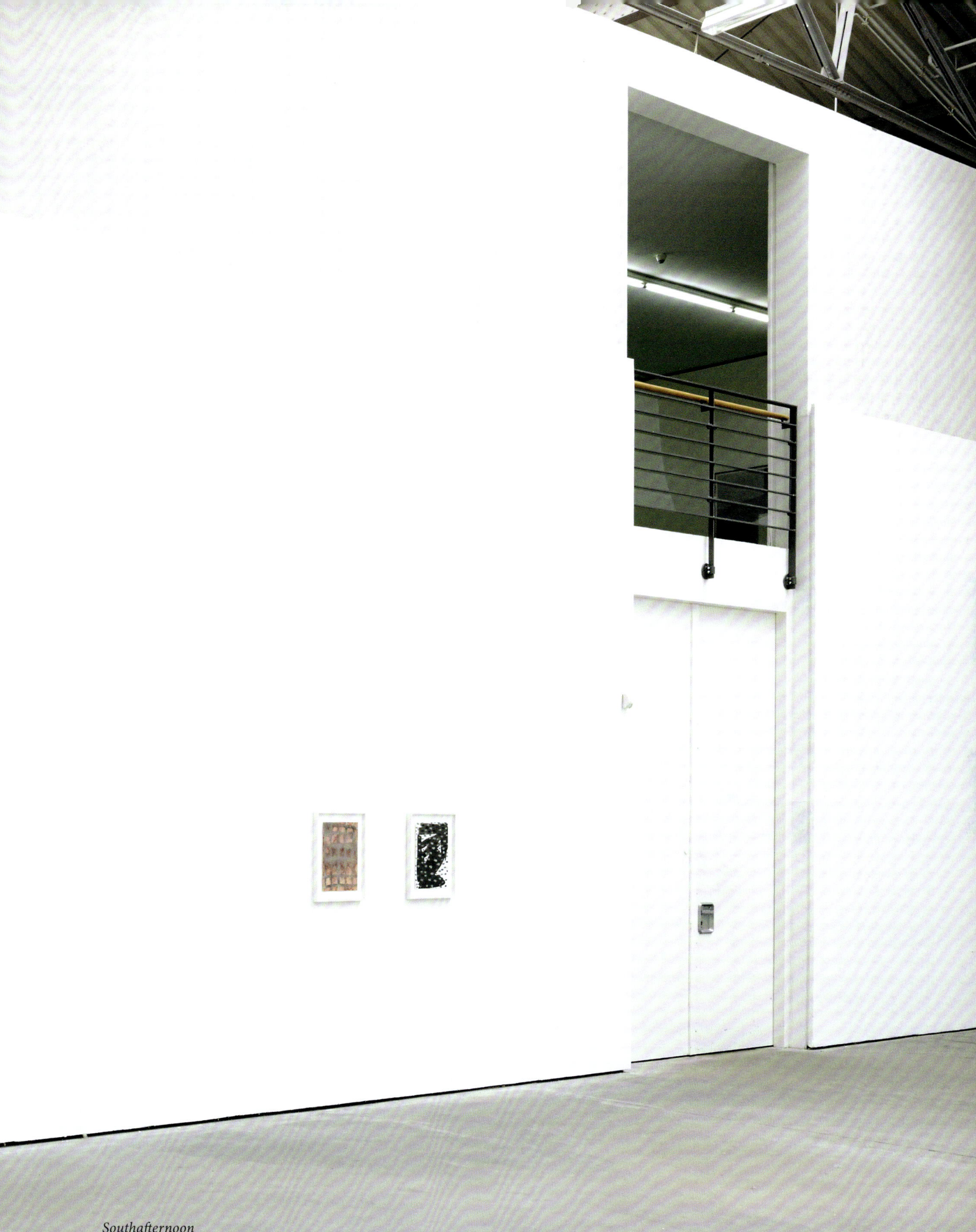

Southafternoon
Ausstellungsansicht / Installation view
Kunsthalle Lingen, Lingen, 2013

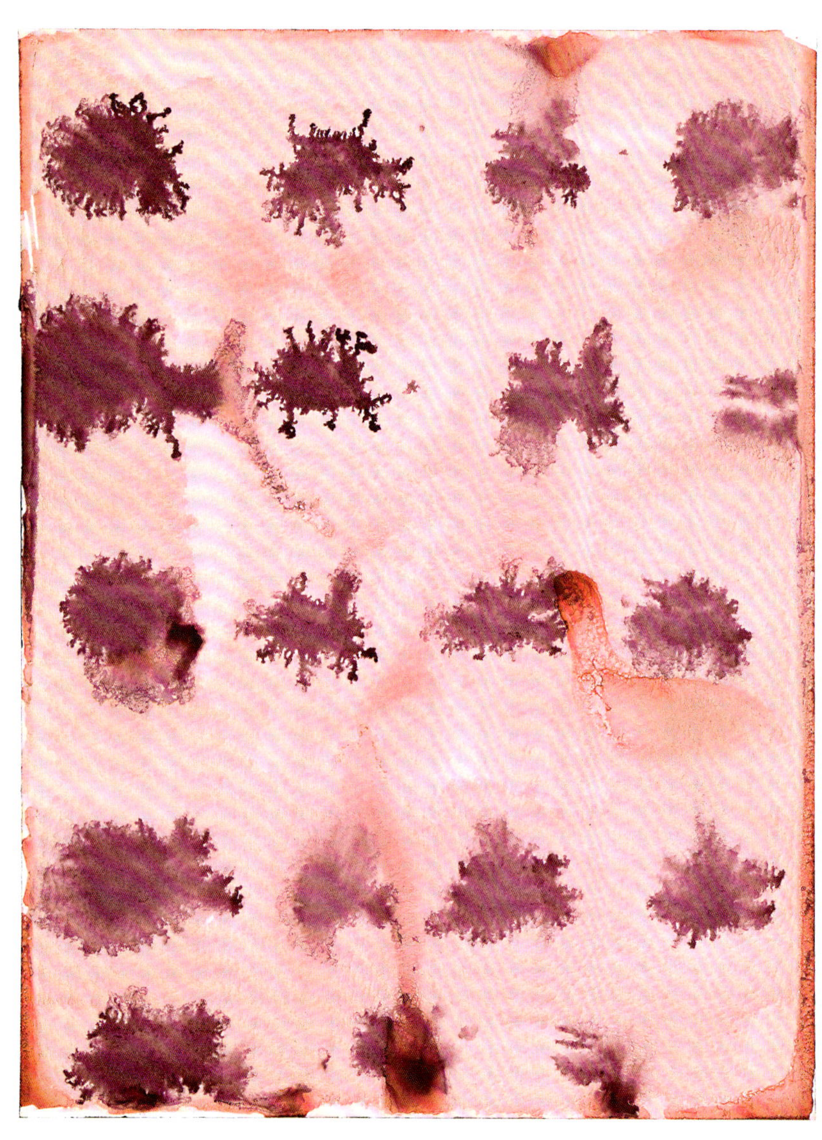

Untitled (#184-12), 2012

Aquarell und Tinte auf Papier / Watercolor and ink on paper 40 × 30 cm / 15 ¾ × 11 ¾ in

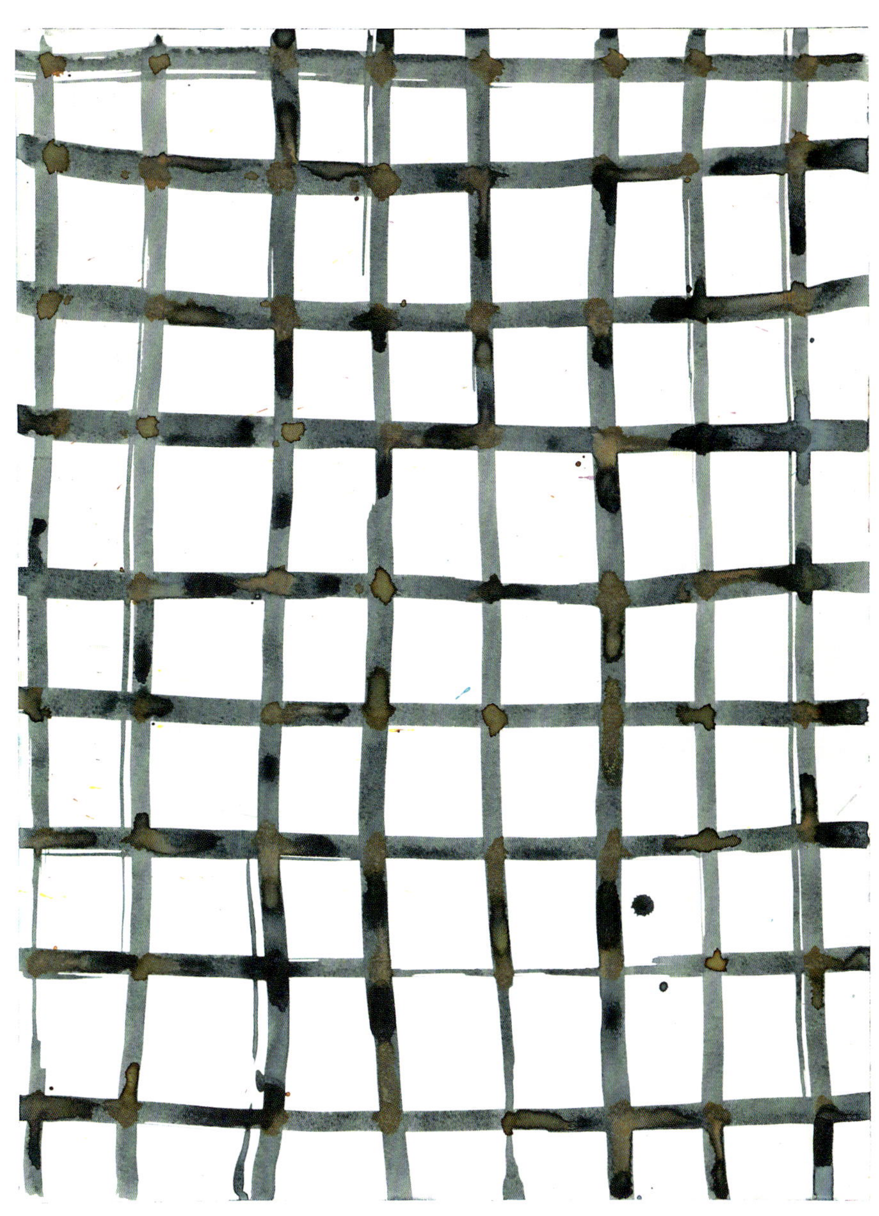

Untitled (#112-12), 2012
Aquarell und Tinte auf Papier / Watercolor and ink on paper 56 × 42 cm / 22 × 16½ in

Untitled (#143-12), 2012
Aquarell und Tinte auf Papier / Watercolor and ink on paper 51 × 36 cm / 20 × 14¼ in

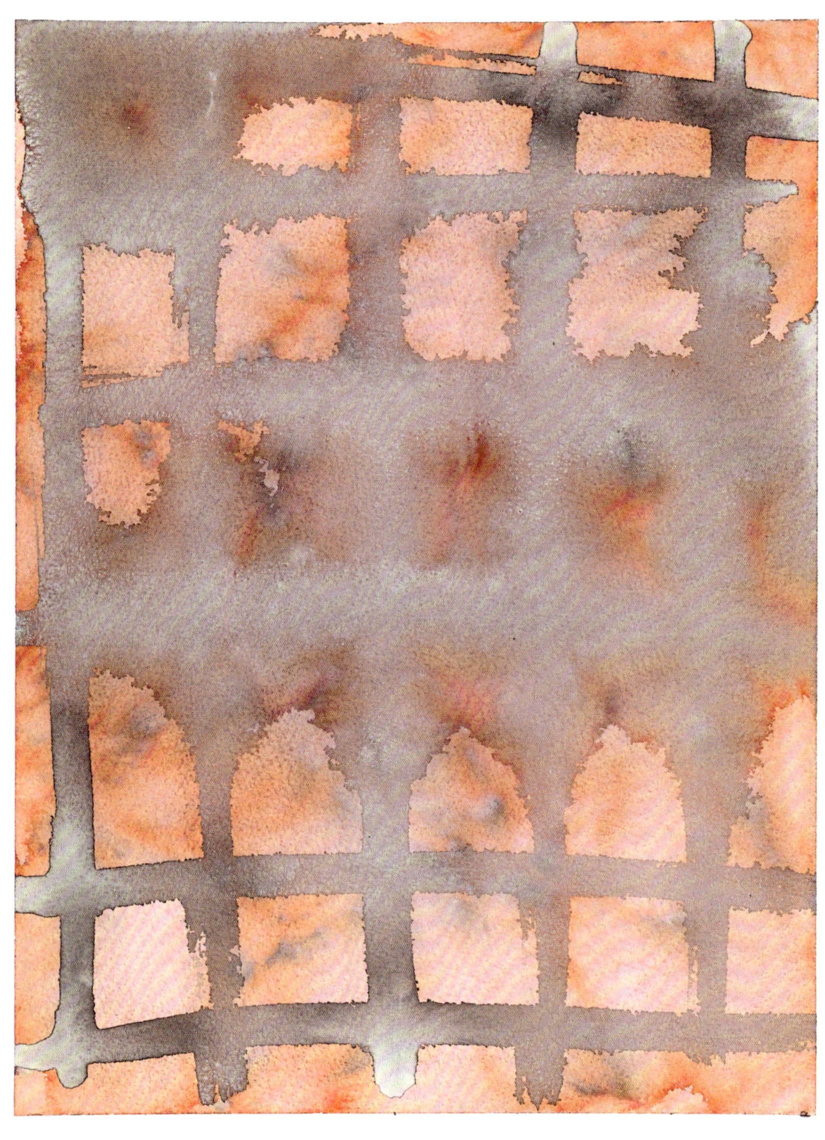

Untitled (#166-12), 2012
Aquarell und Tinte auf Papier / Watercolor and ink on paper 41 × 31 cm / 16 × 12¼ in

Rebecca Morris

1969 geboren / born in Honolulu, Hawaii
Lebt und arbeitet / lives and works in Los Angeles

Ausbildung / Education

1994
The School of The Art Institute of Chicago, Chicago, M.F.A.
The Skowhegan School of Painting and Sculpture, Skowhegan

1992
The School of The Art Institute of Chicago, Chicago: Post Baccalaureate Studio Certificate
Smith College, Northampton, MA: B.A.

Stipendien/Preise / Fellowships/Awards

2013
California Community Foundation Fellowship for Visual Art, Los Angeles
C.O.L.A., Individual Visual Artist Fellowship, Department of Cultural Affairs, City of Los Angeles

2008
John Simon Guggenheim Memorial Foundation Fellowship, New York

2005
The Durfee Foundation, Artist's Resource for Completion Grant, Santa Monica

1999
Louis Comfort Tiffany Award, New York

1996
Art Matters Inc., New York
Special Assistance Grant, Illinois Arts Council, Chicago
Community Arts Assistance Project Grant, The City of Chicago Department of Cultural Affairs, Chicago

Schriften / Writing

2013
„Raoul De Keyser 1930–2012", Passages, ArtForum, März / March, S. / p. 49
Rebecca Morris: 500 words, edited by Zachary Cahill, www.artforum.com, 6. September / September 6, 2013

2012
Grabner, Michelle et al., ON PTG. Oak Park: Poor Farm Press, 2012

2004
MANIFESTO (For Abstractionists and Friends of the Non-Objective)
„The Best of The Best-Ofs", von / by Rebecca Morris, Cakewalk, Ausgabe / Issue 6: 2004, S. / pp. 45–47

1997
„Programming Attitude: An Interview with Laura Owens" von / by Rebecca Morris, Art Muscle, Februar/März / February/March, Band / Vol. 11, Ausgabe / Issue 3

Kuratorische Projekte / Curating

2011
Talks on Painting Lecture Series, organisiert mit / organized with Mari Eastaman und / and Jill Newman, „Intervening in the Picture Plane", „Painters Beyond Painting", „The Pendulum Swings", The Mandrake Bar, Los Angeles

2006
„Jim and Rebecca ♥ Painting", Pasadena City College Art Gallery, Pasadena, Ausstellungskuratorin mit / exhibition curator with Jim Morphesis

2003
Masterminds, Shane Campbell Gallery, Oak Park

Künstlerresidenzen / Residencies

2005
Djerassi Resident Artists Program, Helen L. Bing Fellowship, Woodside

Arbeiten in öffentlichen Sammlungen / Works in Public Collections

The Museum of Contemporary Art, Los Angeles
The Museum of Contemporary Art, Chicago
Sammlung Goetz, München / Munich
Bonnefantenmuseum Maastricht

Einzelausstellungen (Auswahl) / Solo Exhibitions (Selection)

2014
Southafternoon, Bonnefantenmuseum Maastricht
Fantastic L.A., LA><ART, Los Angeles

2013
Party Cut, Corbett vs. Dempsey, Chicago
#18, Galerie Barbara Weiss, Berlin
Southafternoon, Kunsthalle Lingen, Lingen

2012
Works on Paper, Harris Lieberman Gallery, New York

2010
Rebecca Morris, Harris Lieberman Gallery, New York

2009
Shards and Skywindows, Galerie Barbara Weiss, Berlin

2007
Los Angeles, Karyn Lovegrove Gallery, Los Angeles

2006
For Abstractionists and Friends of The Non-Objective, Galerie Barbara Weiss, Berlin
Straight to Hell, Samson Projects, Boston

2005
Rebecca Morris: Paintings 1996–2005, The Renaissance Society at The University of Chicago, Chicago

2004
Rebecca Morris, Susanne Vielmetter Los Angeles Projects, Project Room, Los Angeles

2003

Frankenstein, The Santa Monica Museum of Art, Project Room, Santa Monica

2001

Three-Peat, Boom, Oak Park

RJM 2001: New Drawings, Project Room, Ten In One Gallery, New York

2000

New Paintings, Ten In One Gallery, New York

1998

Rebecca Morris II, Ten In One Gallery, Chicago

1996

Rebecca Morris, Ten In One Gallery, Chicago

Recent Paintings, Galeria Ray Gun, Valencia

Gruppenausstellungen (Auswahl) / Group Exhibitions (Selection)

2014

2014 Whitney Biennial, The Whitney Museum of American Art, New York

2013

Made in Space, Gavin Brown's enterprise and Venus Over Manhattan, New York

C.O.L.A. Visual Artist Fellowship Exhibition, Los Angeles Municipal Art Gallery, Barnsdall Park, Los Angeles

Made in Space, Night Gallery, Los Angeles

The Room and Its Inhabitants, Susan Hobbs Gallery, Toronto

2012

Phantom Limb: Approaches to Painting Today, Museum of Contemporary Art, Chicago

Viva la Raspberries, Harris Lieberman Gallery, New York

Text, Textile, Texture, Galerie Barbara Weiss, Berlin

The Happy Fainting of Painting. Zwischen Bild und Buch: Materialsammlung Malerei heute

Zwinger Galerie, Berlin

2011

Channel to the new image, Friedrich Petzel Gallery, New York

Painting … EXPANDED, Espacio 1414, Santurce, Puerto Rico

La Californie, Public Fiction, Los Angeles

Los Angeles Museum of Ceramic Art at ACME, Acme Gallery, Los Angeles

Dorothea, Ancient & Modern, London

2010

SENT BY MAIL, Galerie Barbara Weiss, Berlin

Ambigu, Kunstmuseum St Gallen, St Gallen

ON PTG: Rebecca Morris, Molly Zuckerman-Hartung and Jutta Koether, Rowley Kennerk Gallery, Chicago

2009

Constellations: Paintings from the MCA Collection, Museum of Contemporary Art Chicago, Chicago

Tables and Chairs, D'Amelio Terras, New York

The Ballad that Becomes an Anthem, ACME, Los Angeles

Sarah Cain & Rebecca Morris, Fellows of Contemporary Art, Los Angeles

2008

The Mystery of the Invisible Clock, Hudson Salon, Los Angeles

Color Climax, James Graham & Sons, New York

Affinities: Painting in Abstraction, Berrie Center for Performing and Visual Arts: Kresge & Pascal Galleries Ramapo College of New Jersey, Mahwah, New Jersey

2007

Albrecht Schnider. Rebecca Morris, Sergej Jensen, Grieder Contemporary, Küsnacht / Zürich / Zurich

ab-strac-tion, Michael Kohn Gallery, Los Angeles

Space is a Place, Portland Institute for Contemporary Art, Portland

The Good, The Bad and The Ugly, New Langton Arts, San Francisco

Affinities: Painting in Abstraction, Hessel Art Museum, Annandale-on-Hudson, New York

Radiant City, Cherry and Martin, Los Angeles

Between the Clock and the Bed, Dave Patton Gallery, Los Angeles

2006

Abstract, Mitchell-Innes & Nash, New York

Selections from My Wardrobe, Karyn Lovegrove Gallery, Los Angeles

Figures in the Field: Figurative Sculpture and Abstract Painting from Chicago Collections, The Museum of Contemporary Art, Chicago

(Keep Feeling) Fascination: Recent Abstract Painting in Los Angeles, The Harriet & Charles Luckman

Fine Arts Complex, California State University, Luckman Gallery, Los Angeles

Ragged, Kate MacGarry, London

2005

The Early Show, White Columns, New York

Sugartown, Participant Inc. (with Elizabeth Dee Gallery), New York

Diamond Hand Grenade: Katherine Bernhardt, Rebecca Morris, Anna Sew Hoy, Midway Contemporary Art, Minneapolis

Abstraktes, Galerie Barbara Weiss, Berlin

2002

Summer: Rebecca Morris, Mary Weatherford, Erik Parker, Tony Gray, Echo Park Projects, Los Angeles

2001

Sound, Video, Images and Objects, Donald Young Gallery, Chicago

Part II: Rebecca Morris, Mari Eastman, Amy Wheeler, Three Day Weekend, 1234 El Paso Drive, Los Angeles

More! More! More! 5117 Eagle Rock Blvd., Los Angeles

2000

Part I: Rebecca Morris, Mari Eastman, Amy Wheeler, Three Day Weekend, 1234 El Paso Drive, Los Angeles

The Windmills of Your Mind, Three Day Weekend, The Royal College of Art, London

The Revolutionary Power of Women's Laughter, China Art Objects Galleries, Los Angeles

1998

Cool Painting, Brian Gross Fine Art, San Francisco
Home-Grown Cool, Wake Forest University Fine Arts Gallery, Winston-Salem, North Carolina

1997

10,000 Lincoln Cheese Logs: Something Different from Minnesota, Illinois and Wisconsin, Wriston, Wisconsin
Post-Pop, Post-Pictures, The Smart Museum of Art, Chicago
B.Y.O.B., Chicago Project Room, Chicago

1996

A–OK, 1223 N. Wolcott, Chicago
Pistoleros de Rayos, Galeria Ray Gun, Valencia

1995

The Uncomfortable Show II, Tough Gallery, Chicago
Skew: The Unruly Grid, Gallery 400, The University of Illinois at Chicago, Chicago
Renee Dryg, Rebecca Morris, Margaret Welsh, Ten in One Gallery, Chicago

Bibliografie / Bibliography

2013

Rebecca Morris bei Barbara Weiss in Berlin, www.kunstmarkt.de, 28. August / August 28, 2013
Rebecca Morris, Party Cut, Ausst. Kat. / exh. cat. Corbett vs. Dempsey, 6. September – 19. Oktober / September 6 – October 19, 2013
Griffin, Jonathan. *Made in Space*, Art-Agenda, http://www.art-agenda.com, 2013
Peipon, Corrina, *Rebecca Morris: Some Observations*, C.O.L.A. 2013, City of Los Angeles Individual Artist Fellowships Katalog / Catalogue, 2013, S. / pp. 60–64
Theiling, Caroline, Malerei und Schwarz-Weiß-Fotografien in der Lingener Kunsthalle, Lingener Tagespost, 21. Mai / May 21, 2013
Rebecca Morris at Kunsthalle Lingen, www.contemporaryartdaily.com, 25. Juni / June 25, 2013
Russeth, Andrew, *Made in Space at Gavin Brown's Enterprise and Venus Over Manhattan*, http://galleristny.com, Juli / July, 2013
Smith, Roberta. *Made in Space*, The New York Times, 1. August / August 1, 2013

2012

Grattan, Nikki, *Rebecca Morris*, http://www.inthemake.net/Rebecca-Morris, 2012
Hix, Mark, und / and Jennifer Higgie, *Valeria Napoleone's Catalogue of Exquisite Recipes*, Köln / Cologne 2012
Shaw, Michael, *Rebecca Morris: An Abstraction Manifesto and How to Be Your Own Jury*, The Conversation: An Artist Podcast, http://theconversationartistpodcast.podomatic.com
Washburn, Stephanie, *Risk, Failure, and the Conventions of Taste, An Interview with Artist Rebecca Morris.* Zócalo Public Square, http://zocalopublicsquare.org
Makers: Women Who Make America, an initative between PBS and AOL. http://www.makers.com/rebecca-morris

2011

Butler, Sharon L., *Abstract Painting: The New Casualists*, The Brooklyn Rail, Juni / June, 2011
Smith, Roberta, *Rebecca Morris*, The New York Times, Freitag, 7. Januar / Friday January 7, 2011, S. / p. 26
Wagley, Catherine, *Can I Have Your Autograph, Peter Voulkos? Five Young Artists and the L.A. Legends They Idolize*, LA Weekly, Art Issue, 23.–29. September / September 23–29, 2011, S. / p. 13
Wilson, *Michael. Rebecca Morris, Harris Lieberman*, ArtForum, Februar / February, 2011, S. / p. 228

2010

Asfour, Nana, *An Artist Who Believes in Painting with a Capital P*, Time Out New York, Ausgabe 795 / Issue 795, 17. Dezember / December 17, 2010
Bitterli, Konrad, Ausst. Kat. / exh. cat. *Ambigu: Zeitgenössische Malerei zwischen Abstraktion und Narration /Ambigu: Contemporary Painting Between Abstraction and Narration*, Kunstmuseum St. Gallen, Schweiz / Switzerland, 2010, S. / pp. 13–14, 48
Elms, Anthony, *Anthony Elms on Rebecca Morris*, Harris Lieberman Gallery, 2010
Thorpe, Vanessa, *Valeria Napoleone: Why She Only Collects Women's Art*, www.guardian.co.uk / The Observer, 17. Oktober / October 17, 2010
Spence, Rachel, *The Female Gaze Of Valeria Napoleone*, Financial Times / Arts Section, London, 13. Oktober / October 13, 2010, S. / p. 2
Zipperstein, Bari, *ShopTalk #13: Rebecca Morris*, http://sidestreet.org/podcasts/rebecca-morris/, 14. Dezember / December 14, 2010

2009

Holte, Michale Ned, *Boofthle Booth-Booth: Deux Doox – The Hollywood Biennale*, Artforum, April / April, 2009, S. / p. 196
Tattersall, Lanka, *Friendly Gestures*, Texte zur Kunst, September / September, 2009, S. / pp. 155–157
Rinder, Laurence, *Raoul De Keyser und die amerikanische Malerei / Raoul De Keyser's American Impression*, Ausst. Kat. / exh. cat. *Raoul De Keyser Replay*, Kunstmuseum Bonn, 2009, S. / pp. 109–112
Archey, Karen, *Do Canaries have accents? Notes from Berlin: Rebecca Morris*, ART FAG CITY, 2. Juli / July 2, 2009
Maak, Niklas, *Manisch malerisch*, FAZ, 3. Mai / May 3, 2009, S. / p. 18

Herold, Thea, *Mandala Melange,* artnet, 5. Mai / May 5, 2009

Schad, Ed, *The Ballad That becomes An Anthem,* ARTsland, 5. April / April 5, 2009

2008

Brooks, Amra. *Art to Live For: our favorite shows and artifacts,* L.A. Weekly, 28. Dezember 2007 – 3. Januar 2008 / December 28, 2007 – January 3, 2008, Band / Vol. 30, Nr. / No. 6, S. / p. 52

2007

Brooks, Amra. *Must See Art,* L.A. Weekly, 28. September – 4. Oktober / September 28 – October 4, 2007, Band / Vol. 29, Nr. / No. 45, S. / p. 54

Holte, Michale Ned, *On the Ground: Los Angeles,* Artforum, Dezember / December 2007, S. / p. 289

Myers, Terry, *Save the Last Dance for Me,* London: Afterall, 2007, S. / p. 84

Brooks, Amra, *Must See Art,* The L.A. Weekly, 4.–10. Mai / May 4–10, 2007, Band / Vol. 29, Nr. / No. 24, S. / p. 58

Weldon, Michael, *Abstract,* The New Yorker, 8. Januar / January 8, 2007, S. / p. 14

2006

Kushner, Rachel, *On the Ground: Los Angeles,* Artforum, Dezember / December, 2006, S. / p. 255

Rossman, Sasha, *Regional Roundup: Berlin,* www.artinfo.com, 6. Oktober / October 6, 2006

Altman, Anna, *Berlin Rising,* www.artnet.com/magazine, 30. August / August 30, 2006

Sew Hoy, Anna / Morris, Rebecca, *Diamond Hand Grenade,* Textfield IV, Frühjahr und Sommer / spring and summer, 2006, S. / p. 58

Joyce, Julie, *(Keep Feeling) Fascination,* Luckman Gallery, Cal State LA, California, 16. März – 6. Mai / March 16 – May 6, 2006

Rebecca Morris Paintings: 1996–2005, The Renaissance Society at The University of Chicago, Chicago, Illinois, 8. Mai – 19. Juni / May 8 – June 19, 2005 Katalog / Catalogue. Essays von / Essays by Diedrich Diederichsen und / and Stephen Westfall

2005

Artner, Alan G, *Seeing Morris' Abstract Growth,* Chicago Tribune, 12. Mai / May 12, 2005, Abschnitt / Section 5, S. / p. 3f.

Hixson, Kathryn, *Rebecca Morris,* Time Out Chicago Ausgabe / Issue 14, 2.–9. Juni / June 2–9, 2005, S. / p. 53f.

Hamza Walker, *Abstract This,* The Renaissance Society, Chicago, Illinois

2004

Ra, Karen, *Contemporary* LA, DOVE Magazine, Korea, Januar / January, 2004, S. / p. 139f.

2002

Charley Magazine, Ausgabe / Issue 1, contributing artist, S. / p. 283f.

2001

Campbell, Shane, *Sound, Video, Images and Objects,* Flash Art, Juli – September / July – September, 2001, S. / p. 70f.

2000

Erickson, Karl, *Three Day Weekend,* Flash Art, November – Dezember / November – December, 2000, S. / p. 51

1999

Eastman, Mari, *My Friend Rebecca,* Cakewalk, Winter / winter, 1999, S. / p. 45–47

1998

Baker, Kenneth, *Cool Paintings Radiate Heat,* San Francisco Chronicle, 12. Dezember / December 12, 1998

Brunetti, John, *Home Grown Cool,* Wake Forest University Fine Arts Gallery: Winston-Salem, North Carolina, 19. Oktober – 15. November / October 19 – November 15, 1998

Grabner, Michelle, *Lake Breeze,* New Art Examiner, September / September, 1998, S. / pp. 22–26

White Walls, Chicago, Illinois, front and back covers, Ausgabe / Issue 40, Frühjahr / spring, 1998, S. / pp. 100–107

1997

Wasserman, Nadine, *Points of Interest … don't laugh,* Wriston Art Center: Appleton, Wisconsin, 27. September – 2. November / September 27 – November 2, 1997

Smith, Courtenay, *Post-Pop,* Post-Pictures, Smart Museum: Chicago, Illinois, 22. August – 21. September / August 22 – September 21, 1997

Hixson, Kathryn, *Feminine Wiles,* New Art Examiner, März / March, 1997, S. / pp. 21–24, 56

Saltz, Jerry, *Uncomfortable,* Time Out New York, Ausgabe / Issue 97, 31. Juli – 7. August / July 31 – August 7, 1997, S. / p. 40

1996

Bulka, Michael, *A-OK,* New Art Examiner, Dezember/Januar / December/January, 1996/1997 S. / pp. 35–36

Walker, Hamza, *All That Glitters is Glitter,* Ten In One Gallery: Chicago, Illinois / Galeria Ray Gun: Valencia, Spanien / Spain, 6. September – 12. Oktober / September 6 – October 12, 1996

Impressum / Colophon

Dieser Katalog erscheint anlässlich der Ausstellung *Southafternoon* von Rebecca Morris vom 18. Mai bis 28. Juli 2013 in der Kunsthalle Lingen und vom 25. April bis 22. Juni und 4. Juli bis 7. September 2014 im Bonnefantenmuseum Maastricht.
This catalogue is published on the occasion of the exhibition *Southafternoon* by Rebecca Morris 18 May to 28 July 2013 at Kunsthalle Lingen and 25 April to 22 June and 4 July to 7 September 2014 at Bonnefantenmuseum Maastricht.

Kunstverein Lingen Kunsthalle
Kaiserstraße 10a
49809 Lingen (Ems)
Fon +49-(0)591-5 99 95
info@kunsthalle-lingen.de
www.kunsthalle-lingen.de

Direktorin / Director
Meike Behm

Ausstellung / Exhibition

Kuratorin / Curator
Meike Behm
Assistentin der Direktion / Assistant Director
Maria-Anna Berlage

Bonnefantenmuseum Maastricht
Avenue Céramique 250
6201 BS Maastricht
Fon +31-(0)43-329 01 90
info@bonnefanten.nl
www.bonnefanten.nl

Direktor / Director
Stijn Huijts

Ausstellung / Exhibition

Kuratorin Zeitgenössische Kunst / Curator Contemporary Art
Paula van den Bosch

Das Bonnefantenmuseum Maastricht erhält langfristige finanzielle Unterstützung von der Provinz Limburg, BankGiro Loterij, DSM und dem Mondriaan Fonds. Das Museum möchte allen Förderern und Freunden des Bonnefantenmuseums Maastricht für ihre Unterstützung danken.
The Bonnefantenmuseum Maastricht receives long-term financial support from the Province of Limburg, BankGiro Loterij, DSM and Mondriaan Fund. The Museum wishes to thank all loaners and friends of the Bonnefantenmuseum Maastricht for their support.

Katalog / Catalogue

Herausgeber / Editors
Kunstverein Lingen Kunsthalle,
Bonnefantenmuseum Maastricht

Lektorat / Copyediting
Meike Behm, Benjamin Chaffee, Julia Hendrickson, Daniel Herleth, Ingrid van Rooij, Kirsten Wandschneider
Übersetzungen / Translations
Jane Yager (Text Meike Behm, Vorwort / Preface), Laura Watkinson, Susanne H. Karau (Text Paula van den Bosch), Nikola Heinrichs (Text Corrina Peipon)

Fotonachweis / Photo Credits
Seite / Page 10: Hilma af Klint, © Stiftelsen Hilma af Klints Verk. Foto / Photo Moderna Museet/Albin Dahlström
Seite / Page 18: Carolee Schneemann, courtesy die Künstlerin / courtesy of the artist, Foto / Photo Shelley Farkas-Davis
Seite / Page 18: Rebecca Morris, Foto / Photo Tom Van Eynde
Seite / Page 18: Jackson Pollock, © 1991 Hans Namuth Estate, courtesy Center for Creative Photography, University of Arizona, Foto / Photo Hans Namuth
Seite / Pages 12, 22–23, 54–55: Roman Mensing/artdoc.de
Seite / Page 48: Fredrik Nilsen
Seite / Pages 24, 26, 28, 30, 32, 34, 36, 38: Lee Thompson
Seite / Pages 8, 40, 42, 44, 46, 50, 52, 56–59: Jens Ziehe
Seite / Page 2, Cover: Rebecca Morris

Gestaltung / Design
Knut Wiese, elfzwei

Bildbearbeitung / Image processing
elfzwei

Druck / Printing
Medialis, Berlin

Auflage / Print run
1.100

Wir danken allen Leihgeberinnen und Leihgebern dafür, dass sie ihre Werke für die Zeit der Ausstellung im Bonnefantenmuseum Maastricht zur Verfügung stellen.
We thank all lenders for providing their works for the time of the exhibition at Bonnefantenmuseum Maastricht.

Untitled (#05-09): Michael Käfer
Untitled (#05-11): Privatsammlung / Private collection
Untitled (#07-11): Privatsammlung / Private collection, courtesy TAJAN SA
Untitled (#03-13): Sammlung Berezdivin / Berezdivin Collection, San Juan, Puerto Rico
Untitled (#04-13): Miriam Lazoff und / and Danny Koplowitz

Dank / Acknowledgements
Die Kunsthalle Lingen dankt / Kunsthalle Lingen thanks: Stiftung Niedersachsen, Anton Mayrose GmbH & Co. KG, Roggendorf fine art – master packer GmbH, Niedersächsisches Ministerium für Wissenschaft und Kultur, Stadt Lingen (Ems), Landkreis Emsland, BP Lingen, Kulturstiftung Heinrich Kampmann.

Alle Werke / All works courtesy Galerie Barbara Weiss, Berlin

Zuerst erschienen bei / First published by
Koenig Books, London

Koenig Books Ltd
At the Serpentine Gallery
Kensington Gardens
London W2 3XA
www.koenigbooks.co.uk

Printed in Germany

Vertrieb / Distribution

Deutschland und Europa / Germany & Europe
Buchhandlung Walther König, Köln, Ehrenstraße 4, 50672 Köln, Fon +49-(0)221-20 59 6-53, Fax +49-(0)221-20 59 6-60, verlag@buchhandlung-walther-koenig.de

Grossbritannien und Irland / UK & Ireland
Cornerhouse Publications, 70 Oxford Street, Manchester M1 5NH, Fon +44-(0)161-200 15 03, Fax +44-(0)161-200 15 04, publications@cornerhouse.org

Außerhalb Europas / Outside Europe
D.A.P. / Distributed Art Publishers, Inc. 155 6th Avenue, 2nd Floor, New York, NY 10013, Fon +1-(0)212-627 19 99, Fax +1-(0)212-627 94 84, eleshowitz@dapinc.com

ISBN 978-3-86335-563-0